PRENTICE HALL
CUSTOM BUSINESS RESOURCES

Compiled by

Negotiation and Conflict Resolution
Cardinal Stritch University

Director of Database Publishing: Michael Payne
Senior Sponsoring Editor: Robin J. Lazrus
Development Editor: Catherine O'Keefe
Assistant Editor: Ana Díaz-Caneja
Operations Manager: Eric M. Kenney
Production Product Manager: Jennifer Berry
Cover Designer: Renée Sartell

This special edition published in cooperation with Pearson Custom Publishing.

Printed in the United States of America.

Please visit our web site at *www.pearsoncustom.com*

Attention bookstores: For permission to return unused stock, call 800-777-6872.

ISBN–13: 9780536836564

ISBN–10: 0536836566

Package ISBN–13: N/A

Package ISBN–10: N/A

PEARSON CUSTOM PUBLISHING
75 Arlington St., Suite 300
Boston, MA 02116

Contents

MAPO City of Metropolis Negotiation

DEC v. Riverside

MOUNTAIN VIEW FARM

Confidential Instructions for the Farmer

You are a third-generation dairy farmer in a small community in northern Vermont. You manage a herd of thirty milking Holsteins as well as a few pigs and chickens for family use. Your land— although a far cry from the flat riverbottom land along the Connecticut River, where you have to look hard to find a stone bigger than your fist—has been good to you. In the fifteen years since you took over from your father, you have managed to double your milking herd and replace the older Jersey cows with better-producing Holsteins.

Although you don't have any big complaints, you are feeling that you have reached the limit as far as what your eighty acres of grazing land can sustain. You have thought about starting a small maple syrup operation now that a gallon of Grade A syrup is selling for more than $24. One good-size maple (between one and two feet in diameter) will often throw off 50 gallons of sap in a year, which boils down to about 1-1/2 gallons of syrup. In addition, you have seen the firewood business in your area take off now that woodstoves are back in style. In Vermont a cord of split and seasoned wood sells for $70–$90 depending on the season, while in Boston the going price is $150.

You already have much of what you would need for both the maple syrup and firewood businesses: more than enough storage space, an old truck that you use to haul things around the farm, a maple sugar house up on the western edge of your property by your father's log cabin (with a little work both could be made usable), a chainsaw, and three different axes with an assortment of wedges. You actually enjoy working with your chainsaw -- although you usually put cotton in your ears when you are using it -- but you hate splitting wood by hand. You have a friend in town who has offered to rent you his automatic woodsplitter for $25 a day, which would both increase productivity and reduce your workload, but you consider that to be too costly. Unfortunately, the small woodlot you have behind your fertile vegetable garden was heavily logged for timber just fifteen years ago. It will be at least another fifteen years before it is producing anything large enough to tap for sap or cut for cordwood.

You have also thought about expanding your herd, but that would mean clearing and fencing more pasture acreage and finding more tillable acreage for hay and silage -- acreage you don't have. What woods you could turn into pasture are steep and rocky, and the costs involved in cutting and burning the brush, removing the stumps, and reducing the acid content of the soil make the whole project of dubious worth.

Recently, you have been thinking about leasing Maggie Anderson's 80 acres of pasture and 20 acres of hayfields, which are available about two miles down the road to the south. The land fits your needs except for its location. You hesitate to get involved in a situation where you will have to manage operations at two separate sites, especially now that your children are gone. The inconvenience costs concern you -- moving your cows back and forth between the two locations could be problematic. Furthermore, Maggie is asking $25 an acre per year for the hayfields and $1 an acre per month for pasture, a price that you cannot afford at this time.

You need to find extra money to pay your taxes, however, and you are considering taking a $9 an hour part-time job snowplowing for the town. You also considered the possibility of renting out your children's rooms in the back part of the house during the winter when they are away at college. People coming up from New York and Boston are willing to pay handsomely for lodging in ski country. That part of the house is expensive to heat in the winter and has a separate entrance and staircase, which would make it attractive to renters. However, somehow you don't like the idea of sharing your house with other people seven days a week, and so you would only consider this as a last resort.

Just when you were ready to forget about expanding the farm, you got a call last week from your neighbor to the west, who comes up from Boston occasionally for summer and winter weekends. Four years ago this neighbor bought the one hundred and twenty acres bordering yours with plans to build a vacation home, but none ever materialized. Your neighbor wanted to know if you would be interested in leasing the entire property on a year-to-year basis.

You would be very interested in leasing the land for a reasonable rent. You could use the 35 acres of hayfields immediately. If the thirty-five acres of hilly land were fenced, it would be adequate for pasturage. Fencing, however, would run about $2,000 for that big a job, and thus it wouldn't be worthwhile to fence on the basis of only a short-term lease. Unless, perhaps, you could cut cedar fence posts on the owner's land, which would reduce the cost to about $400 -- the price of barbed wire and staples.

Another possibility would be to work out some arrangement regarding firewood. The owner's woodlot has some good quality hardwood that needs thinning, and he might be willing to let you cut just enough to pay for the cost of fencing the pastureland. Assuming you could also cut the fenceposts on his land, you estimate that you would only need to cut ten cords to cover the costs of wire and staples, gas and oil for your truck and chainsaw, and renting the woodsplitter. Of course, if the owner expected you to pay for the right to cut the wood, you would need to cut more to cover that expense too. You estimate that two acres would yield ten cords of thinned hardwood.

However, the owner's idea of a fair price is roughly $6,000. You were surprised to hear it, and suggested that $6,000 would be a fair selling price but that $600 is more of what you had in mind for an annual lease. You feel $600 is about what you would be willing to pay for use of the hayfields, though you would be willing to come up a bit, as the land abuts yours and is far more convenient to your herd than Maggie's. The owner was also surprised to hear your estimate of the value of a lease, but you both scheduled a meeting for tomorrow morning to see if the two of you could hammer out a more mutually satisfactory agreement on the price.

MOUNTAIN VIEW FARM

Confidential Instructions for the Owner

You are the owner of 120 acres of land in northern Vermont, which you bought four years ago with your savings of $38,000 cash. At the time it seemed like a good idea. Although there are no buildings on the land, it is part of an old farm with beautiful rolling fields, 50 acres of woods, and on the highest ground, a magnificent building site with a glorious mountain view. A small stream crosses the lower part of the land with an acre or so of flat-bottom land. You visualized building a house on the best site, which you would use for skiing and summer vacations and rent out when you were not using it. You also planned to save on heating bills in your regular home near Boston by cutting fire wood in the winter and bringing it down in your station wagon. You also foresaw savings on food bills by having a vegetable garden on the bottom land near the stream. You were sure that the land would go up in value over time, so that all told, the farm looked like a great investment.

It has not worked out that way. The cost of building even a modest house on the site is much more than you had assumed. Even drilling a well at the site is estimated to cost about $3,000, with no guarantee of hitting water. A road up to the site would be about a third of a mile long—impassable in winter unless you hired someone to keep it plowed. This would cost perhaps $250 for each season. Even then, the road might well be impassable by car during the spring thaw.

You had not thought through just how you were going to use the house for skiing weekends and rent it to others. Local people do not, it turns out, want to rent such a remote house during the winter months. Young people might be persuaded to housesit for you, adapting to your schedule, but not to pay rent. With the additional problems of getting electricity to the site, and keeping the heat on all winter or draining the plumbing every time you leave, you have abandoned any plans to build a house. You did plant a vegetable garden each of the past three springs, at a substantial cost in time and effort, but you found that each summer you got up to the farm on far fewer weekends than you expected. The result was that the weeds took over and eliminated everything except the tomatoes, the zucchini, and some corn. You have eaten so much zucchini, prepared in so many ways, that you can now hardly stand the sight of it. The few ears of corn you grew were delicious but cost about a dollar a cob.

The tomatoes were good and well appreciated, but even they needed a little more attention than they got. The firewood situation is no better. You enjoy the exercise, but your productivity is not what you expected. You love to split wood with your maul and wedges but hate the sound of chainsaws. However, getting the wood prepared for splitting is at least half the job and not using a chainsaw seems admittedly foolish. The chainsaw you need costs around $300, an investment that is hard to justify given the expected $55 of annual savings on your heating bill and the fact that you can buy a cord of well-seasoned firewood in Boston for $140–$150. Furthermore, it is a three-hour drive up to the farm from Boston -- average round-trip gas costs alone are $20. Some winter weekends you have left Boston early Saturday morning, driven up, hiked in the woods and cut firewood for two days, spending Saturday night in a rental cottage about 12 miles away. The cottage is pleasant but expensive, charging ski-weekend prices of $55 on Saturday night. When the weather is nice, you and your friends tend to prefer cross-country skiing to cutting wood. And even when the wood gets cut, it is a long haul to the road. Carrying it by hand in the summer is terrible work. Hauling it on a toboggan in the winter seems to work best, but that time of year the station wagon is always full of ski equipment. Last winter a nice pile of firewood left by the road in February had almost all been stolen by the time you brought your empty station wagon up in the spring.

For the past two summers you have camped on the land in a tent for a two-week vacation. The fields are beginning to grow into brush. The mountain view is becoming obstructed by the young cedar trees that have been sprouting up faster than ever during the past four years. But you do not have the appropriate equipment to clear the fields, and the last thing you want to do is invest any more of your money in this land.

The property taxes on the land went up this year to $780. As an economic matter, the tomatoes and the firewood are hardly worth that. Much as you enjoy cross-country skiing in the winter and camping in the summer, it does not seem to make sense to have so much money tied up in an asset that produces nothing but tax bills. You are certain that the land is an excellent long-term investment. As long as it is used in a way consistent with maintaining the land's value, you would consider leasing the land for whatever it will bring. A few years' rent would allow you to make some improvements: a dirt road could be cut through the woods, or the fields could be moved.

A couple of phone calls to local real estate brokers were of little use. They did not know of anyone interested in renting land but suggested $20–$25 an acre was a pretty standard rate for hayfields.

You figure the land is currently worth $60,000–70,000. A fair rental would be 10% return on your investment after property taxes. You would consider accepting less as long as you did not feel you were being taken.

The farmer whose land lies just to the east of yours keeps pigs, chickens, and cows. Thinking that the hayfields might be of interest to him, you phoned several days ago and said that you were interested in leasing the whole tract of 120 acres for a year, perhaps two, provided that no animals damaged the place and no timber was cleared. The farmer did not quibble with any of your terms and in fact expressed an interest in leasing the land. However, when you mentioned that you thought $6,000 was a fair price, his response was that $6,000 would be a fair price, for an outright sale, but a reasonable year's rent would be more like $600. You expressed as much shock at the low figure as the farmer did at your opening proposal. You said, however, that you would be content with a fair price and would be perfectly happy to sit down together and work one out.

Following the phone call, you did further research on the rental value of land. Apparently the 50 acres of woods have no rental value aside from timber rights. (Because the trees are good-size hardwoods, mostly sugar maple, you could expect to get $400–$600 an acre for the rights to clear them. But an expanse of ugly stumps is not what you had in mind.) Rights to selectively thin out old and crooked trees seem to sell for $200–$250 an acre. According to the county forester, an acre of your woodland would yield about five cords of thinned hardwood, and this would leave the woods in good condition. Aside from cutting a reasonable amount for firewood, you would prefer to leave the woods intact.

Of your 70 cleared acres, perhaps only 35 are level enough to support hay. The other 35 acres are hilly and might be usable as pasture if they were fenced. One thing is for sure, you are not about to sink more capital into the place.

You figure you won't be able to get as much for the place as you had initially hoped. If you and the farmer cannot agree on a price, you may be able to rent the 35 acres of hayfields to someone for $20 an acre. Your local lawyer in Barre has said that all she needs is the lessee's name, the amount of rent, and the length of term, to draw up a standard form lease. Her fee for that would only be $25. Anything more complicated will probably require billing at her hourly rate.

You and the farmer have agreed to meet in the morning to see if you can agree on a price.

THE POWERSCREEN PROBLEM
General Instructions

HackerStar, Inc., is a small, closely held corporation that develops and markets software for microcomputers. It was founded six years ago by Alan Hacker, a trained programmer who brought to the company its first product and became its manager, and Stanley Star, a dentist who has provided the capital. Hacker and Star are each 50 percent owners. The company has always turned a profit, though never a large one, and has appreciated substantially in value. The company is now facing a crisis, however, resulting from a disagreement between the principals over the ownership and disposition of a new product Hacker has developed.

HackerStar's first and still main product is a program called Resource Controller. It is a flexible, multi-purpose tool for controlling peripheral devices of all kinds without extensive custom programming. Its primary uses are in scientific research and small-scale manufacturing, although there are certainly potential home and office applications. First written for the Apple II, it is now available for the IBM PC and other MS-DOS computers, and for the major entries in the Radio Shack line. A version for the Apple Macintosh is under development. Resource Controller is popular among its users, but its installed base of 3,500 users is less than half of the founders' initial expectations, which were:

Year	1	2	3	4	5	6	7
Unit Sales (projected)	750	1,250	2,000	1,500	1,250	1,000	1,000
Unit Sales (actual)	350	448	552	753	696	701	---

Resource Controller retails for $800, and the company actually sees that much if a user buys direct through the mail. If the package is sold through a dealer, there is a 35 percent discount (the industry standard), so the company sees only $520. Schools and charities can buy direct at a 20 percent discount, providing the company with $640.

Just over a year into HackerStar's life, Hacker proposed to Star that he begin work on a second product "to keep HackerStar a growing company." Star, concerned about slow sales of Resource Controller (only 350 packages in the first year), suggested that Hacker's time might be better spent on marketing but finally agreed reluctantly to Hacker's proposal. This second product was PortaWord, a straightforward, "what-you-see-is-what-you-get," word-processing package that works "as is" (except for different disk formats, which are included) on most popular machines. Marketing began halfway through year three. The product is well-designed and has received

This case was written by Bruce M. Patton, Deputy Director of the Harvard Negotiation Project with the help of Mark N. Gordon and Andrew E. Clarkson. Copies are available at reasonable cost from the Program on Negotiation Clearinghouse, online at www.pon.org or by telephone at 800-258-4406.

favorable reviews, but sales revenue didn't catch up with advertising expenses until the beginning of year six. PortaWord retails for $400. Again, the price for a dealer is $260 and for a school or charity is $320.

PortaWord is useful for individuals and larger businesses with incompatible hardware, but market recognition has clearly been a problem. Advertising has been expensive, but used less heavily than Hacker argued it should be. Star, concerned about costs and cash flow, has resisted Hacker's proposals for heavier advertising. He argues that Hacker should push the sales representative to make more of personal contacts with corporate accounts. This basic disagreement about advertising has been a recurring theme between Star and Hacker. Hacker has argued that up to 50 percent more advertising of various kinds would more than pay for itself. Star thinks the risk is too great and the benefits overstated.

In this context, Hacker again proposed at the beginning of year four that he begin development of a new product to position HackerStar to exploit the "nascent but predictable" demand for computer graphics. This proposal, coming only six months after the introduction of PortaWord and at a time when HackerStar's cash flow was at its lowest ebb, greatly concerned Star, who vetoed it. "We need to make the products we have sell before we can afford to think about new ones," he told a disappointed Hacker. He repeated these sentiments on the four or five occasions since then when Hacker again raised the issue, the last time being about six months ago, halfway through year six.

Hacker apparently did undertake efforts to boost sales without additional advertising, because sales of both Resource Controller and PortaWord increased dramatically in year four:

Year		1	2	3	4	5	6
Unit Sales	**RC**	350	448	552	753	696	701
(actual)	**PW**	--	--	14	53	63	85

At the same time, however, Hacker went ahead and began work on a new program, PowerScreen, doing almost all the work in his spare time but making frequent use of (otherwise idle) HackerStar equipment. He finished the bulk of the work on the program halfway through year six and gave Star a quick demonstration after their monthly meeting. Star seemed to think the program was "too esoteric for the business market," however, and he again expressed his displeasure at the prospect of paying to advertise another untried new product.

When Star continued to evidence disinterest in Hacker's new program, Hacker began discussing it with a group of industry venture capitalist friends led by Jeremy Gates whom he met at a computer show. They became seriously interested when they realized the product was essentially complete, and they were enthusiastic when they witnessed a demonstration. They already had plans to set up a software marketing organization to support independently developed programs and thought PowerScreen would be a terrific first product. They proposed an arrangement where Hacker would bear no risk and get a royalty on gross revenue from sales of PowerScreen.

2

Hacker thinks this approach makes good sense and is an eminently fair way to go forward given Star's lack of interest or support. However, when Hacker told him about this proposal, Star was enraged. He argued that PowerScreen was the sole property of HackerStar, both according to the terms of Hacker's employment contract and because Hacker had used HackerStar equipment in developing it. Therefore, he argued that any and all royalties should go to HackerStar and be divided equally. He had no objection in principle to the idea of having Hacker's friends take the risk of marketing PowerScreen. Star's response made Hacker boil in turn. Things went downhill from there.

At a meeting last week between Hacker and Star, an extremely bitter argument between the two occurred. Star accused Hacker of making a deal on PowerScreen behind his back. Hacker told Star that he had offered the program to Star, but Star had rejected it insultingly. As the conversation became increasingly acrimonious, Hacker said, "You have a dentist's mentality. Your wife said that when she split on you . . . . You're an amateur!" Star retorted, "I think you're a child!" The meeting ended with Hacker saying, "Just do something now, quickly, I don't want to talk about this for another six months. Do it now. Dissolve the company, sue me, do whatever you're going to do, just do it now. I just don't want to continue like this, Stan." As Star left the office, he said, "Alan, we're going to have to see you in court and that's not your environment. They don't do things the way you like them in court."

Within hours of their fight, each party independently called the company lawyer to inquire about the law and possible litigation. The lawyer, Dale Levinson, said that, in her opinion, the employment contract was ambiguous as to both the question of whether Hacker had "spare time" that might not be covered by the agreement and as to the question of whether this new product developed without the consent of the board of directors, which comprises Star and Hacker, is covered by the covenant not to compete. (The agreement was drawn up by Levinson's predecessor, James Black, whom Hacker replaced in year two because of dissatisfaction with his work.) She also suggested that Star could sue to enforce the contract, with unpredictable results, and that either party could petition under the state corporations statute for an involuntary dissolution of the corporation if he so chose. Dissolution would, of course, cause each party to recognize income at long-term capital gain rates in the amount of the difference between the tax basis in his HackerStar stock and the liquidation value of half of the HackerStar stock.

Finally, Levinson commented on some of the difficulties Hacker and Star might face in litigation. She noted, for example, that, despite her frequent exhortations that the two keep better minutes of board meetings, the official records of the corporation and minutes of board meetings were not very detailed and provided little evidence of the intentions of the principals with respect to products such as PowerScreen and the employment contract generally. Likewise, she pointed out the general lack of records documenting Hacker's work habits or use of equipment.

The above opinions were somewhat reluctantly given and expressly stated to be tentative and not to constitute advice to either party. To avoid a conflict of interest under the Code of Professional Responsibility, Levinson referred Hacker and Star to separate attorneys of their own for advice on how to proceed. Each has met with his lawyer, and the two attorneys have agreed to meet.

3

Background Information on Alan Hacker

Alan began his computer career as a high school student working summers and after school with the time-sharing machines he could get access to at the universities near his home. He sold his first program, which was for inventory control, to a small business as a sophomore in college. By the time he finished his M.S., he was on the university payroll as a consultant and also had consulted to several large New York firms. After graduation, Alan worked for six years for Digital Equipment Corporation as a programmer and customer service representative specializing in the use of the UNIX operating system with Digital's powerful and popular minicomputers.

Alan left DEC 12 years ago to work as an independent consultant. (DEC was a frequent client.) This work produced a steady, but unspectacular income of about $25,000 to $30,000 per year. When the Apple II microcomputer was released three years later, Alan saw great potential in the microcomputer market, and began planning ways to get into it as a software vendor. Star heard about his plans and expressed interest, and they began to explore the possibility of a joint venture. Star had the capital Alan needed, and Alan had the kind of ground-floor product in which Star was looking to invest a modest sum. Within a couple of months, HackerStar was under way.

Background Information on Stanley Star

Stanley is a dentist with a medium-sized solo practice in town. Seven years ago, shortly before the creation of HackerStar, Stanley's wife left him for a stock broker. Having just turned 50, Stanley went through a major reevaluation of his life and career. He decided to ease up a bit on the practice of dentistry and spend his spare time on an exciting new business venture. Stanley began to dabble in real estate investments, followed the stock market with some interest but little success, and spent a couple of months trying to figure out just what kind of serious business endeavor he should embark upon. Although he had no particular business experience other than managing his own investments, Stan believed that he would make a first-rate entrepreneur.

Stanley had accumulated enough capital in years of practice that his savings and investments, even after the divorce settlement, enabled him to put a chunk of his own money into some business enterprise without any significant risk to his financial well-being. It was complete serendipity that Stanley ran into Alan at a computer show just at that time. Stanley had met Alan at a few previous social gatherings, but they were merely casual acquaintances. As soon as Stanley heard that Alan was looking for capital to enter the microcomputer market, he knew that, with Alan's technical capabilities and his own business acumen, a joint venture would be beneficial to both of them. Stanley had always been interested in computers as a hobby and as a tool for keeping track of patient records in his office, so teaming up with a computer whiz like Alan seemed very attractive, especially given the potential for growth in the computer software industry. Stanley thought that HackerStar had the potential for huge financial gain with minimal financial risk and that the company would not require him to divert too much of his energies from his ongoing dental practice.

4

Background Information on HackerStar, Inc.

HackerStar was founded six years ago. Alan Hacker and Stanley Star are the sole shareholders and directors; each holds 50 percent of the company. Star provided initial capital of $65,000 and loaned the company an additional $30,000 (at nine percent interest) at the beginning of year three. Interest is paid monthly; none of the principal has been repaid. HackerStar's note to Star is a demand note; no demand for principal repayment has ever been made.

Hacker has an eight-year employment contract with the company (attached). He is assisted by one sales representative, Jim Sparks, who works on a straight salary. Hacker is quite satisfied with Sparks' work. Star is more skeptical about Sparks' performance, but he spends too little time in the office to have much concrete basis for his concerns other than the company's general cash flow. Sparks declined a suggestion in year four that 40 percent of his salary be switched to commission income, although he was willing to accept commissions above his salary and a link between sales and raises in his base salary. No action was taken on his counterproposal, however, because Star was not enthusiastic, and Hacker did not push the issue.

HackerStar uses the David Marks Advertising Agency for copy design and campaign planning. The HackerStar ads generally have a clean design and a good impact. The Marks agency has a good industry reputation.

The company hired an additional programmer, Jay Gould, in year four to help with the conversion of the company's products to new equipment, including new printers. The company also employs two secretaries, Janice Banks and Dorothy Devine. Office equipment and a receptionist are shared with other enterprises in their office complex. The company has no profit-sharing plan. Annual raises are currently running at five percent, although they were as high as seven percent in the first three years of the company when inflation rates were high.

HackerStar's products are sold through mail order advertising in computer magazines, such as *Byte*; through about 20 dealer representatives, mostly Computerland stores; and through direct mail and personal contact with potential buyers. Detailed income and expense summaries for the first six years are attached.

EMPLOYMENT AGREEMENT

This agreement is made this first day of July, [six years ago], between HackerStar, Inc., a corporation existing under the laws of New York, hereinafter referred to as the company, and Alan Hacker, hereinafter referred to as the manager.

Whereas the manager has for a number of years been engaged in the business of computer software design and development for mini– and microcomputers, a business similar to that to be conducted by the company, and whereas the knowledge and skills he has gained in that enterprise are considered essential in conducting the business of the company, it is hereby agreed:

1. The company will employ the manager as its general manager for a period of eight years from this day, at an annual salary of $30,000. It is understood and agreed between the parties hereto that this annual compensation may be altered, revised, or increased by mutual consent of the parties hereto without detriment or prejudice to the remainder of the covenants herein, all of which shall remain in full force and effect until terminated, as provided by this agreement.

2. In consideration of the compensation arrangements hereby covenanted, the manager hereby covenants and agrees to devote his full time, energies, knowledge, and abilities to the management, operation, and development of the business of the company. The manager shall conscientiously and diligently perform all required acts and duties and faithfully discharge all responsibilities entrusted to him as general manager.

3. The duties of the general manager, subject to supervisory approval of the board of directors of the company, shall include the supervision of the company's plant; the purchase, installation, and supervision of equipment; the employing and discharge of employees; the design, placement, and evaluation of advertising; and any and all other duties usually incident to those of a general manager, including such duties as the board of directors of the company from time to time may suggest. No expenditures or liabilities outside of those arising from the ordinary and usual course of business shall be incurred unless the direct approval of the board of directors of the company shall have been first obtained, and all purchases made by said manager on behalf of the company shall be at net cost price. All contracts for salaries of personnel shall be submitted for approval to the board of directors of the company.

4. While the manager is employed hereunder and for one year after termination of such employment, the manager will not (i) engage in competition with the company, either directly or indirectly, in any manner or capacity as advisor, principal, agent, partner, officer, director, stockholder, employee, member of any association, or otherwise in any phase of the business of designing, writing, testing, selling, or producing microcomputer software for the control of peripheral devices or for other such purposes as the company may develop software, and (ii) compete, either directly or indirectly, in any such manner or capacity with any other business of the company in which the manager served while employed hereunder. Ownership by the employee, in the aggregate, of less than one percent of the outstanding shares of capital stock of any corporation with one or more classes of its capital stock listed on a national securities exchange or publicly traded in the over-the-counter market should not constitute a breach of the foregoing agreement.

6

5. This agreement constitutes and expresses the whole agreement of said parties hereto in reference to any employment of the manager by the company and in reference to any of the matters or things herein provided for, or herein before discussed or mentioned in reference to such employment, all promises, representations, and understandings relative thereto being herein merged, unless the terms and provisions of any subsequent employment shall be in writing and duly authorized by the board of directors of the company.

In witness whereof the parties have signed and sealed this agreement this first day of July, (six years ago).

Stanley Star   *Alan Hacker*

Stanley Star   Alan Hacker
Chairman of the Board   President and General Manager
HackerStar, Inc.   HackerStar, Inc

.

HACKERSTAR, INC.
INCOME AND EXPENSE REPORTS

Year 1

Expenses

Hacker	$ 30,000
Sparks	20,000
Banks	10,000
Fringe (20%)	12,000
Office Space	20,000
Phone	10,000
Supplies & Misc.	5,000
Equipment	18,000
Printing	20,000
Disk Mfg.	5,000
Advertising	72,000

Total Expenses   **$222,000**

Income

200 x $800 =	$160,000
100 x 520 =	52,000
50 x 640 =	32,000
Total Income	$244,000
Less Expenses	222,000
Profit	
Before Taxes	$ 22,000
Less Taxes	4,400
Net Income	**$ 17,600**

Year 2

Expenses

Hacker	$ 32,100
Sparks	21,400
Banks	10,700
Receptionist	3,000
Fringe (20%)	13,440
Office Space	16,000
Phone	14,000
Supplies & Misc.	5,500
Equipment	12,000
Printing	5,000
Disk Mfg.	1,000
Advertising	99,000

Total Expenses   **$233,140**

Income

255 x $800 =	$204,000
154 x 520 =	80,080
39 x 640 =	24,960
Total Income	$309,040
Less Expenses	233,140
Profit	
Before Taxes	$ 75,900
Less Taxes	23,624
Net Income	**$ 52,276**

8

Year 3

Expenses

Hacker	$ 34,347
Sparks	22,898
Banks	11,449
Receptionist	3,120
Fringe (20%)	14, 363
Office Space	17,000
Phone	18,500
Supplies & Misc.	6,000
Equipment	13,500
Printing	12,700
Disk Mfg.	3,000
Advertising	169,800
Interest on Loan	2,400
Total Expenses	**$329,077**

Income

288 x $800 =	$230,400
247 x 520 =	128,440
17 x 640 =	10,880
7 x 400 =	2,800
7 x 260 =	1,820
Total Income	$374,340
Less Expenses	329,077
Profit	
Before Taxes	45,263
Less Taxes	8,415
Net Income	**$36,848**

Year 4

Expenses

Hacker	$ 36,064
Sparks	24,043
Gould	24,000
Secretaries	24,020
Receptionist	5,000
Fringe (20%)	22,625
Office Space	18,000
Phone	19,500
Supplies & Misc.	6,000
Equipment	14,000
Printing	22,000
Disk Mfg.	5,000
Advertising	183,000
Interest on Loan	2,700
Total Expenses	**$405,952**

Income

344 x $800 =	$275,200
401 x 520 =	208,520
8 x 640 =	5,120
14 x 400=	5,600
24 x 260 =	6,240
15 x 320 =	4,800
Total Income	$505,480
Less Expenses	405,952
Profit	
Before Taxes	$ 99,528
Less Taxes	33,067
Net Income	**$ 66,461**

9

Year 5

Expenses

Hacker	$ 37,867
Sparks	25,245
Gould	25,200
Secretaries	25,221
Receptionist	5,250
Fringe (20%)	23,757
Office Space	18,500
Phone	21,000
Supplies & Misc.	6,000
Equipment	15,000
Printing	13,700
Disk Mfg.	3,000
Advertising	188,300
Interest on Loan	2,700
Total Expenses	**$410,740**

Income

340 x $800 =	$272,000
350 x 520 =	182,000
6 x 640 =	3,840
33 x 400 =	13,200
20 x 260 =	5,200
10 x 320 =	3,200
Total Income	$479,440
Less Expenses	410,740
Profit	
Before Taxes	$ 68,700
Less Taxes	20,950
Net Income	**$ 47,750**

Year 6

Expenses

Hacker	$ 39,760
Sparks	26,507
Gould	26,460
Secretaries	26,482
Receptionist	5,513
Fringe	24,944
Office Space	19,000
Phone	22,000
Supplies & Misc.	6,500
Equipment	15,000
Printing	12,850
Disk Mfg.	3,025
Advertising	204,125
Interest on Loan	2,700
Total Expenses	**$434,866**

Income

322 x $800 =	$257,600
378 x 520 =	196,560
1 x 640 =	640
36 x 400 =	14,400
49 x 260 =	12,740
Total Income	$481,940
Less Expenses	434,866
Profit	
Before Taxes	$ 47,074
Less Taxes	11,192
Net Income	**$ 35,882**

HACKERSTAR, INC.
BALANCE SHEET
(Fiscal year ending June 30)

ASSETS

Cash	$ 20,765
Short-term Notes	115,000
Accounts Receivable (Net 30 days)	33,560
Inventory	*5,750
Total Current Assets	$175,075
Fixed Assets (Net of depreciation)	124,035
Prepaid Rent	1,880
Total Assets	*$300,990*

LIABILITIES AND EQUITY

Accounts Payable	$ 43,505
Total Current Liabilities	$ 43,505
Stockholder Loan	30,000
Total Liabilities	$ 73,505
Stated Capital	65,000
Retained Earnings	162,485
Total Liabilities and Equity	***$300,990***

*Market value is $120,000.

11

THE POWERSCREEN PROBLEM
CURRENTLY PERCEIVED CHOICE TOOL

[Whom are we trying to influence? What is the primary decision they see themselves facing? From their perspective, what are the pros and cons of that decision?]

DECISION MAKER:_____

QUESTION: Shall I (we)_____

If "YES"	If "NO"
[negative consequences of saying "yes" to the above question, in possible order of importance]	*[favorable consequences of saying "no" to the above question, listed in order of the subjects on the left]*
-	+
-	+
-	+
-	+
-	+
	BUT: *[negative consequences of saying "no"]*
BUT: *[favorable consequences of saying "yes"]*	-
+	-
+	

CURRENTLY PERCEIVED CHOICE TOOL

DECISION MAKER:_____

QUESTION:_____

                                                                        If "NO"

                    If "YES"

                                            +

-

                                              +

-

                                              +

-

                                              +

-

                                              +

-

                                              +

-

                                              +

-

                                              +

-

                                              +

-

                                            BUT:

BUT:

                                              -

+

                                              -

+

                                              -

+

                                                                                2

TARGET BALANCE SHEET

[How would we like, and how can we reasonably expect, the target decision maker to see his choice in the near future? Faced with a new choice (our new proposal), what favorable consequences do we want the decision maker to see if he says "yes"? What negative consequences do we want him to see if he says "no"?]

DECISION MAKER:_____

QUESTION: "Shall I (We) accept their new proposal, the X plan?"

                                  If "NO"

            If "YES"

	−
+	
	−
+	
	−
+	
	−
+	
	−
+	
BUT:	**BUT:**
	+
−	
	+
−	

TARGET BALANCE SHEET

DECISION MAKER:_____

QUESTION: "Shall I accept proposal X?"

<table>
<tr><th>If "YES"</th><th>If "NO"</th></tr>
<tr><td>+</td><td>-</td></tr>
<tr><td>+</td><td>-</td></tr>
<tr><td>+</td><td>-</td></tr>
<tr><td>+</td><td>-</td></tr>
<tr><td>+</td><td>-</td></tr>
<tr><td>+</td><td>-</td></tr>
<tr><td>+</td><td>-</td></tr>
<tr><td>+</td><td>-</td></tr>
<tr><td>BUT:</td><td>BUT:</td></tr>
<tr><td>-</td><td>-</td></tr>
<tr><td>-</td><td>-</td></tr>
<tr><td>-</td><td>-</td></tr>
</table>

4

YESABLE PROPOSITION

[Once we understand the target decision maker's interests and concerns, what proposal can we generate and refine to meet those interests?]

Proposed Action: *Who should do what, when, to address the immediate problem?*

_____

_____

_____

Proposed Action Formulated as a YES or NO Question: *Will you (do)*

_____

_____

_____

Sufficient: *The proposed action is sufficient to deal with the immediate problem because it addresses the following issues within this problem:*

_____

_____

_____

Legitimate: *The proposed action is legitimate for dealing with the immediate problem because it addresses the following issues within this problem:*

_____

_____

_____

Realistic: *There is some reasonable chance they will agree to the proposed action because it meets the following important interests of theirs:*

_____

_____

Operational: *Once they agree to the proposed action, it can be implemented without the need for them to make further decisions. (check)* _____

5

RESTRAINTS ON CHOICE

[Even if our yesable proposition meets the target decision maker's interests, that decision maker will face restraints on his or her choice to say "yes" because of criticisms from third parties and/or constituents.]

If the target decision maker agrees to our proposal, his worst responsible critic (one whose opinions can't easily be ignored) might say:

"_____

_____

_____ "

[In order to persuade our target decision maker, it is useful to draft a possible response to that criticism.]

Our target decision maker can respond persuasively, "This is the best decision for us because

_____

_____

_____ "

THE POWERSCREEN PROBLEM
Confidential Instructions for Alan Hacker's Attorney

You are a partner in a small local law firm. One of your law school classmates, Dale Levinson, called to ask if she could refer a client to you. She has been representing HackerStar, Inc., for more than four years.But now that there is a problem between the two principals in that company, she feels she should bow out and has recommended that each retain separate counsel. You agreed to talk with one of the principals, Alan Hacker. In the course of a client interview, you found Hacker to be eccentric, clever, and likeable. Hacker seemed to feel that he had been wronged by his partner, Stanley Star. It also appeared that constraints on his creative energy were really troubling him. The following is a summary of what you learned from Hacker in preparing for your upcoming meeting today with Stanley Star's attorney.

For Alan Hacker, starting his own software house was always a dream but one he never had the capital to realize on his own. When Star came along as a possible backer, things finally seemed to fall into place. Hacker had some concerns, of course. Star knew just enough about computers and the industry to understand his ideas but not enough to realize he really didn't know anything important. Hacker had worried that Star might try to force the company to follow some foolish ideas of his own—for example, he once mentioned a screenplay-writing program when he and Hacker were first talking about setting up the company—but that is one thing he has been pretty good about.

On the other hand, your client feels that Star never has understood HackerStar's need for advertising. According to Hacker, Star just looks at advertising as throwing money down a black hole and doesn't seem to grasp that you can get the money back, often in ever-increasing amounts, once you break a certain threshold of market recognition. Star also doesn't understand how important it is to accomplish that early on, before the market gets saturated with competitors. Hacker claims that Star has never understood that market penetration is highly volatile, that high-tech industries such as microcomputer software represent fading opportunities, and that the longer you wait to gain market recognition, the less your market share is likely to be for any given product.

According to Hacker, Star thinks HackerStar's failure to achieve its early sales projections is Hacker's problem. Hacker's response is that, while he may not be the world's best salesperson, he is not totally incompetent or he would never have made it in business on his own for six years. Hacker argues that the money saved by not hiring an extra manager increased the revenue available for additional advertising, which paid for itself two-fold by generating additional sales.

This case was written by Bruce M. Patton, Deputy Director of the Harvard Negotiation Project with the help of Mark N. Gordon and Andrew E. Clarkson. Copies are available at reasonable cost from the Program on Negotiation Clearinghouse, online at www.pon.org or by telephone at 800-258-4406. This case may not be reproduced, revised, or translated in whole or in part by any means without the written permission of the Director of Curriculum Development, Program on Negotiation, Harvard Law School, 518 Pound Hall, Cambridge, MA 02138. Telephone: 617-495-1684, Fax: 617-495-7818. Please help to preserve the usefulness of this case by keeping it confidential. Copyright ©1984, 1990, 1995, 2004 by the President and Fellows of Harvard College. All rights reserved. (Rev. 03/04).

Your client seems amazed at the position Star is taking on the PowerScreen program. He doesn't see how Star can justify having his cake and eating it too. Star told him he wasn't interested in the program six times, that it was not marketable, that HackerStar couldn't afford it anyway, and that he couldn't work on it on company time. Then he turned around and claimed that the company owned it! Hacker admits he spent 200 or so hours on the company minicomputer using its sophisticated debugging program that simulates an IBM PC, but he claims he did it late at night and on weekends when no one else needed the machine. Hacker indicates that total development time was approximately 2,000 hours but that the bulk of that time was spent writing code on his personal computer. He says he would not have worked those hours and had no need to work those hours except for his desire to write this program. Your client insists that he did everything else he could to see to the continued best marketing of HackerStar's existing products.

Hacker thinks that Star is just mad at being wrong. He knows that Star is disappointed in the company's performance and that Star attributes this to a lack of effort on the part of Hacker and Jim Sparks. Your client, on the other hand, attributes it to a lack of support for adequate advertising, especially in the first few years of operation. Now the market is so saturated with advertising that it is hard to get any attention. When HackerStar was just starting, however, an extra $50,000 might have made a big difference. Instead, Star insisted that the company make a profit from the first year. In Hacker's opinion, that is why sales are lower than the company's early projections indicated they would be.

Hacker acknowledges that it must "burn" Star to think of a new income stream coming in and HackerStar not getting it, especially because it was his own decision not to pursue it. But as far as your client is concerned, he did everything conceivable to satisfy his duty of loyalty to HackerStar. He offered the company both the idea and the finished product, and he made no effort to pursue other channels until the company expressed its disinterest finally and unequivocally. Once the company did so, he proceeded to rely on that lack of interest. Consequently, he feels that he should derive the benefit from his unsupported work to develop the program and to find backers for it.

As far as the covenant not to compete in his employment contract goes, Hacker argues that it just does not apply. He explained to you that a graphics program is not in any way competitive with a word-processing package or a peripheral control program. Furthermore, the company stated its lack of interest in developing a competitive product. On the question of "full-time energies," Hacker thinks that means the time it takes to do what the company wants to do. He feels he put that time in. As he put it, there are only so many hours in a day when one can call customers and dealers. Any other time is his, and he says he did virtually all of this development work on his own time. Furthermore, he says that not more than 30 hours of thinking were spent during work time to develop PowerScreen, and this occurred only when things were slow. You remain a little skeptical.

If it comes to it, your client would rather cut the company in for ten to 15 percent of the royalties on PowerScreen than see the company fall apart, but he doesn't want to feel taken, especially not

2

by Star. After all, Hacker thinks this mess is Star's fault. Hacker suggested it would help if an agreement could be reached that the company would support a reasonable number of new products as he develops them and that the company would give him the time and latitude to do so. Indeed, you got a strong sense that creating new products is what Hacker really cares about, that R & D is "where his heart is." After some prodding, you ascertained that, in Hacker's ideal world, he would spend all of his time being a creative genius, working on developing any new programs that struck his fancy. Hacker added, though, that an increase in advertising, especially for new products, would also help.

Your client's backers for PowerScreen, led by Jeremy Gates, have expressed considerable flexibility. They have offered a royalty of five percent of gross sales up to $30,000, seven-and-a-half percent of gross sales between $30,000 and $50,000, ten percent of gross sales between $50,000 and $75,000, and 12.5 percent of gross sales above $75,000. Hacker thinks this is a fair and even generous offer. While he would certainly like to make a lot of money, he seems to be more concerned with having his computer programs recognized and respected than with financial rewards per se.

While Gates and company do intend to set up a software distribution and marketing firm (to be called Software Super Marketing), they might also consider investing in HackerStar directly. If so, your client would want to join them to take control of PowerScreen's marketing away from Star, so he could be sure that his software would be backed properly. If Star raises the possibility, Hacker would like to agree on a package deal for the Gates group to consider. He would also like to agree on what Hacker and Star will do if Gates' group decides they are not interested in anything other than the royalty deal.

Prepare for your meeting with Star's attorney. Hacker wants to avoid litigation and keep the company going if he can, but he doesn't want to feel "ripped-off" by Star. Hacker has given you full authority to develop recommendations and proposals, but he will decide ultimately what he wants to do. It is clear, though, that he will give serious weight to your advice.

3

THE POWERSCREEN PROBLEM
Confidential Instructions for Stanley Star's Attorney

You are a partner in a small local law firm. A friend of yours, Dale Levinson, called to ask if she could refer a client to you. She has been representing HackerStar, Inc. for more than four years, but now that there is a problem between the two principals in that company, she felt she had to bow out and recommend that each retain separate counsel. You agreed to talk to one of the principals, Stanley Star. In the course of a client interview with Star, you found Star to be straight-laced, serious, and apparently honest. The following is a summary of what you learned from Star in preparation for your upcoming meeting with Alan Hacker's attorney.

Your client, who is chairman of the board of HackerStar, Inc., has always been interested in computers as a hobby and as a tool for keeping track of patient records in his practice. When he was looking for a good investment six years ago, backing a start-up software venture seemed natural. Alan Hacker seemed like a good bet. He had a solid professional reputation, a stable client base, lots of experience, and a good product in hand. The figures he presented on potential market and projected sales were impressive. Star's only concerns were whether Hacker had the management and marketing expertise to turn his projections into reality and, if he did have the expertise, whether he would give up programming to do it.

Now it seems that Star's instincts may have been better than his judgment, because it is precisely those concerns that have come to haunt him. When he and Hacker first discussed the possibility of setting up HackerStar, Star suggested that the company should employ a professional manager and marketing person. Hacker was not enthusiastic about the idea, although Star says he could never really tell if this was for business reasons or if it was a matter of pride. What Hacker said was that the money would be better spent on advertising, that he could handle the small staff, and that a good advertising agency could guide the marketing. Star made one last attempt, suggesting that a smart young person just out of a good business school would not cost that much, but Hacker kept talking about how crucial advertising was for a new product. Hacker finally agreed that hiring a sales manager might be a good idea once the company was underway, and Star decided to wait and see.

HackerStar's first year was not an unqualified success. It did make money, which your client realizes is unusual if not unprecedented, but sales were less than half of projections. All year long Hacker wanted to spend more on advertising, even suggesting the company take out a loan to do so, but he never could provide any hard evidence of how much more was needed or how

This case was written by Bruce M. Patton, Deputy Director of the Harvard Negotiation Project with the help of Mark N. Gordon and Andrew E. Clarkson. Copies are available at reasonable cost from the Program on Negotiation Clearinghouse, online at www.pon.org or by telephone at 800-258-4406. This case may not be reproduced, revised, or translated in whole or in part by any means without the written permission of the Director of Curriculum Development, Program on Negotiation, Harvard Law School, 518 Pound Hall, Cambridge, MA 02138. Telephone: 617-495-1684, Fax: 617-495-7818. Please help to preserve the usefulness of this case by keeping it confidential. Copyright ©1984, 1990, 1995, 2004 by the President and Fellows of Harvard College. All rights reserved. (Rev. 03/04).

precisely it would help. Then, suddenly, he told Star that he wanted to write another program, even as the company was struggling to succeed. Star didn't know what to make of it. Hacker's arguments that having a line of products would make the company more secure and generate more recognition among dealers seemed to make sense, but he wouldn't admit that there might be a tradeoff between R & D and current sales. Again, Star says he suggested the need for a sales manager, but Hacker was adamant in his resistance. Hacker wanted the money for advertising, and Star was afraid Hacker might just quit if he didn't get it. Finally, Star just gave up and went along. But he was not happy, and Hacker knew it.

When Hacker came back at the beginning of year four and proposed developing yet another product, your client put his foot down. Sales on both Resource Controller and PortaWord were still way below projections. Star reminded Hacker that Hacker had taken on the job of sales and marketing manager over Star's objections and that it was therefore Hacker's responsibility to see that the job got done right. Star wanted to see increased sales immediately, which took precedence over anything and everything else. At first, he thought that Hacker got the message. But he soon found out that Hacker had just gone right ahead and developed PowerScreen without telling him. Sales did go up in year four but not anywhere near to Hacker's own projections. They went down again in years five and six.

When Hacker finally did tell your client what he had done, Star was not happy. It is clear that PowerScreen is another quality Hacker product with a significant potential market; Star does not dispute this fact. His question is whether its development and marketing by HackerStar really represents a wise business decision.

Like your client, you don't completely believe Hacker's claim that the work to develop PowerScreen was done in his "spare time." Developing a major program like PowerScreen requires a huge creative effort that is bound to be more interesting to someone like Hacker than selling an old idea. Certainly he spent hours daydreaming about PowerScreen instead of selling the company's existing products. Likewise, you have no doubt that Hacker made significant use of company time and equipment to do the work. Hacker admits to using the powerful and sophisticated PC simulator on the company's minicomputer to debug his program. Developing this program probably cost HackerStar money in the form of reduced sales.

As far as your client is concerned, there is no justification for Hacker's claim that PowerScreen is owned by him exclusively. Star's argument is that, no matter what the language of the employment contract, it is perfectly clear that he and Hacker had discussed, intended, and agreed that, in exchange for Star's initial backing of the company, Hacker would owe all of his creative software energy to HackerStar. Under their agreement, Hacker should have had no spare time to develop his own product. According to Star, this agreement is not limited to products that compete directly with existing HackerStar products but applies to all microcomputer software products that Hacker might develop. You pointed out to Star that, on paper at least, the contract was somewhat ambiguous and that there might be problems proving intent. Basically, however, you agreed with his point of view.

2

In addition to the issue of the contract, other issues are Hacker's use of company equipment for PowerScreen's development and the fact that the time he spent seems to have detracted from the success of the company's other products. It is certainly not obvious that a reluctance to go forward in the way Hacker proposed translates into a waiver of his employment contract covenants not to compete and to devote his full energies to the company. You can make an excellent argument that his program is HackerStar's, however it is marketed.

Star thinks Hacker is insulted that he didn't fall head over heels in love with PowerScreen and abjectly admit that he had been wrong not to be interested at first. Star is prepared to apologize if that will help, but it doesn't change the contractual reality. Star has the sense that Hacker doesn't really take his judgment very seriously, that he just wants his money. For example, when they were first talking about creating the company, your client suggested developing a program to help Hollywood screenwriters, but Hacker just laughed it off without ever asking him why he thought such an idea might be worth considering. Hacker's high-handed and devious approach to writing PowerScreen is, Star thinks, an indication of this attitude as well as a good illustration of why it needs to be challenged.

What Star wants to do first is to get Hacker to admit the company owns PowerScreen and then work out an effective way to go forward so that the company handles sales effectively and Hacker doesn't go off on his own again. In Star's view, that almost certainly means it is finally time to hire a real manager and to designate Hacker head of R & D. Hacker could also supervise the other programmer's work keeping old products up to date and compatible with new machines.

Your client wants the company to keep going. Despite the fact that it has not turned out to be the cash cow he was expecting, Star is fond of it and feels that it is a respectable company. With proper sales management and Hacker's ideas, it can do much better. Star would be willing, if necessary, to let Hacker take ten or 15 percent of the royalties if that would allow him to save face. However, your client would want to couple that with a clear understanding that, in the future, all Hacker's work would be owed to the company. Another possible alternative is to have Hacker's venture capitalist backers buy into HackerStar to help with its marketing if they are willing. Star thinks this might be a good option, but he would not want to lose real control. First, though, he wants to get Hacker to calm down and look at things realistically. Your client feels that Hacker's petulance and emotional outbursts are entirely inappropriate in a business context. He insists that Hacker conduct himself reasonably, without venomous name-calling, and look at the situation maturely. If Hacker absolutely won't do this, then Star would rather sue him than be left with the feeling that he had been "ripped-off."

Prepare for your meeting with Hacker's attorney. Basically, your client wants to know how best to proceed, whether litigation is necessary (and if so, with what purpose in mind), or whether something can be worked out without litigation. Star has given you full authority to explore any proposal and develop a recommendation, but he will be the one to decide finally what he wants to do. Of course, he will give serious weight to your advice.

3

SALLY SOPRANO
SOME POSSIBLE CRITERIA FOR ESTABLISHING SALARY

The following are some of the possible standards by which one can establish a salary for Sally in her performance of *Norma*. Note that the first and the last are not independent or objective standards.

STANDARDS	SALARY
What Lyric is willing to pay to get her to sing (?)	$45,000
Last title role in *Norma* x 2 (for inflation in opera salaries) + $1,000 (because time is short)	$45,000
Last title role x 2 (for inflation in opera salaries)	$44,000
Same premium (2.75 x secondary) Sally received 4 years ago when she sang lead	$38,500
Best recent secondary role x 2 (for lead) + some adjustment for inflation	$36,000
What Lyric paid last year's lead + 25% for inflation	$31,250
Sally's last secondary role with the Lyric x 2 (for lead) + 25% (one year's inflation in opera salaries)	$31,250
What Lyric would have paid the other singer	$30,000
Last year's secondary role x 2 (for lead) + 25% (one year's inflation in opera salaries)	$30,000
Less than Lyric would have paid the other singer because Lyric preferred her to Sally	$30,000
Current secondary role x 2 (for lead)	$28,000
Sally's lowest secondary role in the past 2 years x 2 (for lead) + 25% (inflation)	$25,000
What Lyric paid Sally last year (secondary role) x 2 (for lead)	$25,000
Sally's lowest secondary role in the past 2 years x 2 (for lead)	$20,000
Sally's highest most recent (secondary) role	$18,000
What Sally's been willing to sing for in the past 2 years + 50% (inflation)	$15,000
What Lyric paid Sally the last time (secondary role)	$12,500
What Sally's been willing to sing for in the past 2 years	$10,000
What Sally said she'd be willing to sing for (?)	$ 0

SALLY SOPRANO
SOME CREATIVE OPTIONS

(Illustrative components of agreements)

- Percentage of gate to go to Sally:

    X% of excess over average gross ticket sales
    X% of excess over last five operas put on by Lyric
    X% of ticket revenues after Sally's name is publicly announced
        minus average ticket sales in three weeks prior to opening
    X% of ticket revenues over Lyric's break-even point
    After 75% of seats sold for a given performance, X% of ticket
        revenues if house is 75-85% full, Y% of ticket revenues if
        house is 85-95% full, and Z% of ticket revenues if house is
        95-100% full

- Advertising:

    Lyric agrees to $X advertising budget
    Lyric agrees to increase existing ad. budget by $X (or X%)
    For every three dollars increase in the Lyric's advertising budget,
        Sally will contribute a dollar to the Lyric (subject to ceiling
        of $X contribution by Sally)
    Sally and her agent get input into content of ad campaign
    Sally gets superstar comeback buildup in Lyric's advertising

- Superstar perks for Sally:

    Enormous limo for Sally during entire run of *Norma*
    Dressing room and hospitality room, each with big star on door,
        fully stocked with goodies
    Dozens of roses to be thrown up on stage by adoring fans (to be
        planted by Lyric) after each performance
    Huge opening night gala, complete with show-biz stars,
        searchlights, and lots of media

- Sally and Lyric agree to create records and tapes of performance; cut deal
    on royalties and jointly negotiate with recording company

- Sally and Lyric agree to pack first three rows with enthusiastic fans each night to precipitate tumultuous ovations

- Sally agrees to conduct masters classes at the Lyric, locking in long-term employment for Sally and opera world notoriety for Lyric

- Sally agrees to specifically plug the wonderful people at the Lyric on national prime-time TV if the television deal comes through

- Lyric agrees to hire the best make-up artist in the business to make Sally appear youthful and vibrant

- Lyric agrees to pay Sally $100,000 for role (payable over 20 years, so present value is about $20,000)

- Lyric pays Sally $45,000 and she agrees to contribute half to Lyric's newly-established "Sally Fund" to aid struggling young sopranos

- Sally sings for nothing in charity run of *Norma* and Lyric contributes all net proceeds to Sally Fund

- Lyric pays Sally $45,000 and she agrees to match dollar for dollar any corporate contributions to Sally Fund which are raised by the Lyric's Business Manager

- Sally gets an extra $5,000 and agrees to buy any unsold tickets at half the box office price (up to a ceiling of $10,000) and arrange for distribution of those tickets to students in arts programs, retirement homes, widows, orphans, etc.

2

SALLY SOPRANO I

SAMPLE PREPARATION MEMO

ISSUES TO BE CONSIDERED

1. Salary

2. Publicity

  - What will Lyric do?

  - What could Sally do?

3. Future contracts between Sally and Lyric

4. Rehearsals

5. Work-related benefits and incentives, e.g., flowers in dressing room, limousine

6. Joint ventures e.g., create records and tapes of performance

7. Other joint gains?

SALLY'S ALTERNATIVES

Sally's alternatives to an agreement include:

  - Sit home and watch TV on opening night

  - Hope for the TV special to come through based on her past performances

  - Look for another role

  - Volunteer to teach classes on performing arts to get publicity

Discussion of alternatives from the perspective of Sally's representative:

None of these alternatives is appealing to Sally. She would much prefer reaching an agreement with Lyric. Her BATNA with Lyric seems to be for her to find another role for this season. We must determine how likely such an alternative would be, especially since the season is only three weeks away. Before going into the negotiation, however, I will want to discuss with Sally what might be done to improve her alternatives. For example, could she start talking to other opera companies about roles (hopefully, roles which she already knows) or could she set up a TV or radio interview to discuss her past performances and her upcoming return to the opera world? I would be stronger in the negotiation if Sally and I could improve her BATNA by having already set up another role, even one that she would prefer not to take given the choice between it and the lead in *Norma*.

LYRIC OPERA'S ALTERNATIVES

The Lyric Opera's alternatives to an agreement include:

- Use the inexperienced secondary soprano in the lead role and probably pay her less than $28,000 (twice her salary in the secondary role)

- Look for other lead opera singers

- Cancel the show

- Start a large-scale publicity campaign featuring the secondary soprano

- Start a publicity drive to lower expectations for this season because of Renata Risingstar's sudden unfortunate illness.

Discussion of alternatives from the perspective of Lyric's representative:

Canceling the show right now would be devastating from a financial perspective and from the perspective of the opera's reputation in the operatic community. It is probably too late to find another lead opera singer because all of the good ones would be in rehearsal for other operas. Our BATNA is to use our current secondary soprano in the lead role. This is taking a chance since she lacks experience in demanding lead roles. We should improve our BATNA before going into the negotiation with Sally's agent by starting the secondary singer in rehearsal right away. In fact, tonight I will call the director and voice coach and tell them to start the secondary in rehearsal first thing in the morning.

SALLY'S INTERESTS

Sally's interests include:

- Making a comeback in opera

- Proving to the opera world that she's still good enough

2

- Enhancing her reputation

- Performing a primary role

- Renewing her relationship with the Lyric Opera

- Establishing a precedent of a high salary

- Receiving treatment appropriate to her past fame

Discussion of interests from the perspective of Sally's agent:

Before going into the negotiation, I must prioritize these interests. Sally seems most interested in *getting* the lead role and less interested in what the actual salary is. Of course, I recognize that Sally would be happier singing for more money than for less. She is also concerned, however, that the world views her as a successful and talented star, despite her age and recent withdrawal from the opera world. Since she also wants to get the TV role, any option Lyric's representative and I come up with should take into account how the media and the TV producers will see Sally. Therefore, whatever publicity we can arrange, the better the deal will be. I think that Lyric may have a strong interest in publicity for this last-minute substitution, as well.

THE LYRIC OPERA'S INTERESTS

The Lyric's interests include:

- Successful run of *Norma*

- Establishing the precedent of always paying only the appropriate salary

- Not being taken advantage of

- Use of the best available opera singer

- Good box office sales

- Providing and receiving adequate publicity

Discussion of interests from the perspective of Lyric's representative:

Lyric's highest priority interest is to get the best possible opera singer for the lead role so that the season will be a success. It cannot afford, however, to have opera singers think they can take advantage of Lyric's misfortune by demanding extraordinary salaries in a situation like this where the original star cannot perform. On the other hand, Lyric wants to maintain its reputation of treating its singers fairly. If we reach an agreement with Sally, both parties will have an interest in a successful run of the opera. There also seems to be a shared interest in good publicity for the opera and for Sally.

3

RELATIONSHIP

What interest does each party have in pursuing a good working relationship?

A good relationship will help Sally in her performance, which benefits both parties. Consequently both parties need to be able to work well together during the run of *Norma*. Because a success is important to both, neither party wants to create a situation in which one or the other sabotages the performances.

How should that be reflected in the negotiation?

An ideal negotiation in this situation is an amicable one in which the parties feel like this is a joint problem to be solved by taking into consideration the best outcome for all involved. Pushing to the last dollar could possibly prevent agreement and would be counter-productive since both parties are worse off without an agreement.

What interest do the parties have in a long-term relationship?

The possibility of a long-term contract should be discussed as a future possibility to keep our options open. I should go back to my client to find out if there is an interest in such a contract. That is not crucial to this negotiation, however.

Other long-term relationships could be beneficial to the parties since both Lyric and Sally have a certain amount of fame and expertise. They may be able to help each other out.

COMMITMENT

What would be possible good outcomes of this meeting?

- A firm contract

- An agreement in principle to be shown to Sally and Lyric

- A press release to the media about Sally's comeback and Lyric's new star

In reaching this agreement, the commitment must be:

SUFFICIENT: It must cover all interests such as salary, publicity, etc.
REALISTIC: It must be an agreement that both parties can perform.

OPERATIONAL: Its terms must be such that it can be carried out as soon as the parties sign the contract. Everyone must know exactly what he or she is expected to do.

Among the possible outcomes, I believe my client would prefer a firm contract. I have the authority to commit to a contract for the run of the *Norma* season. I would need to consult with my client before agreeing to anything of a more long-term nature.

COMMUNICATION

I will be much more persuasive if I can show the other party's representatives that I am listening to them and that I understand what they are saying. Once they recognize that I hear them, they can hear what I am saying. If they do not believe that I am listening/understanding them, they will expend all their energy advocating their position, and it will be twice as hard for me to persuade them.

How can I show that I'm listening?

- Paraphrase what they say and repeat it back with: "If I've heard you correctly, I think you've said that…"

- Maintain good eye contact

- Ask questions

- Acknowledge their concerns even if I disagree with them by saying, for example, "I understand why you see this as a problem. Let me add my perception of the situation."

First, it is important for me to remember that I can acknowledge what they say without agreeing with them. Second, I must not lead them to believe that my acknowledgements of what they say mean that I am agreeing with them. For example, if I tend to nod my head when I am listening attentively, I must tell them explicitly that I hear what they are saying but that I do not necessarily agree entirely. Third, by the tone I set in the negotiation, I can disagree without being disagreeable.

5

SALLY SOPRANO I

CONFIDENTIAL INSTRUCTIONS FOR SALLY'S AGENT

You have just become a partner in a firm that manages and acts as agent for celebrities. Sally Soprano is certainly not a major client, but you want to do a good job with this first assignment as a partner, especially since you have an interest in expanding your firm's opera practice. This is the first time you have handled Ms. Soprano's account.

You met Ms. Soprano yesterday. She is an older soprano who still has a good voice, particularly for her age. During your discussions with her, you gathered the following information:

She has not had a prime role in more than two years, although she has had a number of secondary roles. Her popularity has declined somewhat in the past few years. Lyric Opera, with whom Sally has sung many times over the years, has a production of Bellini's *Norma* scheduled to open in three weeks. The challenging title role is generally acknowledged to be a prize for a young soprano. When the Lyric announced this season's schedule over a year ago, Renata Risingstar was listed in the title role for *Norma*. Ms. Risingstar is generally regarded as a first-rate performer, although she has not yet attained the popularity Sally enjoyed at the peak of her career. Three weeks ago, Ms. Risingstar's name was suddenly dropped from the opera's advertising, and rumors began circulating that she had either become ill or gotten into a dispute with the artistic director. Sally got in touch with the artistic director to ask if the title role was open. Sally knows the part well and has sung it successfully many times. Yesterday Sally was informed by the Lyric that they might be interested in signing her for the Norma role. A meeting has been scheduled for today between you, as Sally's agent, and the Lyric's business manager to discuss the situation.

The Lyric Opera is an established institution in a major metropolitan area. As with most opera companies, it is a not-for-profit entity that is financed by a combination of ticket sales, foundation and corporate grants, and income from a modest endowment. It usually breaks even over the course of the year, with fairly good attendance in its 2,000-seat hall. Ticket prices range from $18 to $55. This production of *Norma* is scheduled to run for six weeks, with three performances per week.

Sally desperately wants this role. It could signal a real comeback and would give her a good chance at an important role in a forthcoming television special on opera. The TV special would pay $45,000 and would probably lead to many other singing engagements. Sally was overjoyed at Lyric's possible interest in her. Sally has told you that getting the part is what counts; the amount of compensation is secondary. She told you that, frankly, she would be willing to sing the part for nothing, except for reasons of professional pride, reputation, and the potential impact on future engagements, although the higher the price the better.

Sally's salary over the last two years for secondary roles in operas of this type has ranged from $10,000 to $18,000. Four years ago, when she was at the pinnacle of her career, she received $22,000 for performing the title role in *Norma* at the Lyric. Since then, due to inflation and the increased popularity of opera, the amount paid to top opera singers has nearly doubled. Sally recognizes, however, that she cannot count on producing sold-out performances the way she could then.

Last year, the inexperienced young soprano who sang the title role of *Norma* for the Lyric was said to have been paid over $24,000. The last time Sally sang for the Lyric was over a year ago, in the secondary soprano role of Adalgisa, also in *Norma*, for which she received $12,500 and received reasonably good reviews. Although it is difficult to generalize, performers in lead opera roles of this type are usually paid at least twice the amount received by singers in secondary roles.

Sally believes that her experience and maturity make her particularly appropriate for the title role. Norma is the high priestess of the Temple of Esus. She is secretly married to the Roman Consul and has had two children with him. There are two other sopranos in the opera: Adalgisa, the virgin of the temple, and Clotilde, the attendant to Norma. Sally feels that, given her age, she would no longer be the best person to play the role of Adalgisa or Clotilde. However, she believes that at this stage of her life she relates well to the role of Norma. In fact, Sally's view is that she actually may have been too young when she performed the role of Norma in the past and that she would perform this role better today.

One of the Lyric's major concerns is the attendance Sally's performances would generate. The Lyric is said to average around an 85 percent house over the course of a year, but many performances are sold out. On the other hand, a bad house can be financially devastating for the annual budget. While her voice remains strong, she has had a few mediocre days, which wasn't true four years ago. That is one reason why you think Sally has been offered fewer roles recently. If Sally's performances generated a 50 percent or 60 percent house, this would almost surely be her last leading role. In fact, anything under 80 percent would probably finish her career. Sally is confident, however, that a 50 percent or 60 percent house would be extremely unlikely to occur as a result of *her* contribution.

Prepare for your meeting with the Lyric Opera's Business Manager.

SALLY SOPRANO I

CONFIDENTIAL INSTRUCTIONS FOR LYRIC OPERA'S BUSINESS MANAGER

You have been with Lyric Opera for three months. So far, things have been going well, but your negotiation with Sally Soprano's agent will be your most important assignment to date. You want to make sure that your boss, the artistic director, is pleased with the outcome.

You met with your boss yesterday, and gathered the following information:

The Lyric Opera is an established institution in a major metropolitan area. Like most opera companies, it is a not-for-profit entity and is financed by a combination of ticket sales, foundation and corporate grants, and income from a modest endowment. It usually breaks even over the course of the year, with fairly good attendance in its 2,000-seat hall. Ticket prices range from $18 to $55, with $28 a reasonable average for rule-of-thumb accounting.

A production of Bellini's *Norma* is scheduled to open in three weeks. The production is scheduled to run for six weeks, with three performances per week. There are three sopranos in *Norma*. Norma is the high priestess of the Temple of Esus and is secretly married to the Roman Consul, with whom she has two children. The other two soprano roles are those of Adalgisa, the virgin of the temple, and Clotilde, the attendant to Norma. The challenging title role is generally acknowledged to be a prize for a young soprano, although the age of the character is not specified. The age of the children is also unspecified, but Norma attempts to kill them in a rage over her husband's infidelity.

When the Lyric announced this season's schedule more than a year ago, Renata Risingstar was listed in the title role for *Norma*. Ms. Risingstar is generally regarded as a first-rate performer, although she has not yet attained the popularity Sally enjoyed at the peak of her career. Three weeks ago, however, the Lyric suddenly dropped Ms. Risingstar from its advertising for *Norma*. Although it is not widely known (the opera wanted to hold off making a public announcement until the diagnosis was confirmed), the reason for the omission is that Ms. Risingstar has developed a benign throat tumor that will require surgery prior to the performance date. The Lyric has been unable to find any other good soprano who is available for the dates of the performance. The soprano engaged for the secondary role (at a salary of $14,000) knows the *Norma* role. She has a good voice but is a relative newcomer to professional opera and clearly lacks the experience necessary to perform the title role well. The Lyric is therefore in a tight spot. Cancellation of the opera would result in a loss of hundreds of thousands of dollars. Fortunately, Sally Soprano, a distinguished though somewhat aging soprano, heard rumors that the opera was in trouble and called the artistic director to inquire whether there was any possibility that she might sing the lead. Up to now, the artistic director has held her off, hoping to find a younger lead. Unfortunately, that now appears impossible, and the artistic director is suddenly quite desperate to sign Sally. You have scheduled an early appointment with her agent.

Sally Soprano has sung many times for the Lyric Opera over the years, but the last time she sang was more than a year ago in the secondary role of Adalgisa, also in *Norma,* for which she received $12,500. Four years ago, at the pinnacle of her singing career, the Lyric paid Ms. Soprano $22,000 for performing the title role in *Norma.* That was regarded as extremely high at the time, justified only by the fact that Sally was at the apex of her career and had a significant following, which has probably fallen off somewhat since then. On the other hand, over the last four years, inflation and the increased popularity of opera have in general brought about a near doubling of the average salaries of the top opera stars.

As a matter of policy, the Lyric does not generally disclose the compensation of its performers. However, for negotiating purposes, you have been given access to the salary figures paid by the Lyric in recent years for the title and secondary roles in Bellini's *Norma:*

	Title Role (Norma)	Secondary Soprano (Adalgisa)
Five years ago	$14,000	$7,000
Four years ago	$22,000	$8,000
Three years ago	$17,500	$9,000
Two years ago	$21,000	$12,500
Last year	$25,000	$12,000
This year	?	$14,000

Although cases vary widely, as a general rule the Lyric tends to follow the industry practice of paying performers in lead opera roles of this type about twice the amount received by singers in secondary roles. Also, following the industry practice, the Lyric has always paid its performers a flat rate salary.

In general, the nonprofit Lyric needs to keep the costs of performances as low as possible. The Lyric's average house over the year is generally 85 percent. This is also the break-even point. Of course, there have also been many sold-out performances, but the average is 85 percent, give or take five percent. Anything less than 80 percent attendance would cause the Lyric to lose $50,000 or more, and a house of 50 percent or 60 percent, while unlikely, would be a disaster. (These kinds of figures probably explain why Ms. Soprano has had so few offers for lead roles recently. While her voice remains fine, most operas are anxious to avoid even the smallest chance of an off day.)

This year, Ms. Risingstar was to have been paid $30,000. In view of the emergency situation and the great desire of the artistic director to obtain Sally Soprano, the Lyric trustees have authorized you to offer her up to $45,000 should that be necessary. If she holds out for more than that, the Lyric will just have to use the neophyte secondary soprano in the title role and hope that she miraculously rises to the occasion. (You would probably pay her something less than double her secondary salary of $14,000 for that, certainly no more than $28,000.) You should also bear in mind the potential adverse impact on future negotiations with other performers should an unusually high salary for Sally become public knowledge.

The artistic director wants Sally, despite thinking that she is too old for the role. The director believes that with proper makeup and a little luck Sally could work out extremely well. In any event, there is little alternative. As it is, the late announcement of the title role may adversely affect box office sales. The artistic director is hoping, however, for a favorable public response to the announcement of Sally in the title role.

Prepare for your meeting with Sally Soprano's agent.

MAPO
CITY OF METROPOLIS NEGOTIATION

General Information

This negotiation involves discussions between the Metropolis Association of Police Officers (MAPO) and representatives of the City of Metropolis from the office of Mayor H. Holmes. The issues to be negotiated pertain to the City's budgetary allocations for the next fiscal year—"Year 0." The negotiation will be closed to the public, but each participant must be aware of the ever-present potential for selective "leaks" to the media by individuals on either side of the negotiation.

Metropolis is a large American city. With a total of 712,000 residents enumerated in the most recent census, Metropolis is the 14th largest city in the United States. In terms of area, it is the 24th largest. The population of Metropolis has been growing at an annual rate of a little over two percent. Despite this marginal growth in population, the tax base in Metropolis has diminished slightly in each of the last three years due to an exodus of businesses from the downtown area. A comparative study of housing, food, and miscellaneous living expenses ranked Metropolis as the seventh most expensive city in the nation. Inflation in Metropolis this year matched the current national rate of approximately *twelve percent*. Appendix A contains certain demographic statistics for Metropolis and the six other major urban centers in the region.

In the last election, voters in Metropolis narrowly failed to approve "Proposition 6," which would have limited municipal budget increases for any department to a maximum of 6% over the previous year's allocation. Proposition 6 is again on the ballot for the elections to take place in just over two months. If recent polls and media analyses are correct, it appears that Metropolis voters are about to approve Proposition 6 overwhelmingly.

Despite the trend in parts of the country toward collectively-bargained, multiple-year contracts between police departments and city administrations, formal collective bargaining in Metropolis' budget formulation process has not been pervasive in the past. Each group of municipal employees has some form of association, but only the teachers are formally unionized and part of a national organization. All other municipal workers' associations have had regular contact with Metropolis officials and have obtained agreements regarding budgetary allocations, but have not obtained contracts *per se* with the City. These agreements usually cover only the budget for the next fiscal year; the City has been unwilling to commit itself to agreements of greater duration.

In contrast, the Metropolis Teachers Union has successfully negotiated four successive two-year contracts with the City. MAPO has had informal contact with the Mayor's administration in the past, but has never before conducted comprehensive negotiations relating to the Police Department budget and other police issues.

Briefly summarized, the budget process involves three stages. First, the Mayor negotiates with representatives of each municipal department over the budget for that department. Assuming they agree on a figure, the Mayor then submits this recommendation to the City Council for its approval. Holmes, a former member of the Metropolis City Council, enjoys an excellent relationship with a majority of the council, and in most cases Holmes's budget recommendations have been approved with only minor changes. The City Council then returns the budget to the Mayor for signature. The Mayor has a final veto over the City Council's budget appropriation, but exercise of this veto power has never proved to be necessary.

The Police Department of Metropolis has an authorized strength of 1000 persons. (See Appendix B for police department statistics from Metropolis and six other cities in the region, as well as comparable information for the Metropolis Fire Department.) The Metropolis police force is currently staffed at a level of 976 officers due to budgetary constraints and a chronic shortfall in the number of new recruits entering the Police Academy. The budget for the Police Department in the current fiscal year is $61,875,000, which represents about 12% of the total Metropolis budget. This figure represents a per capita expenditure on police well below the national average for cities the size of Metropolis. (See Appendix C for nationwide police personnel statistics.) The starting salary for a member of the Metropolis police force is $22,500 and the maximum salary is $29,500. For these salaries to equal the median level for cities of comparable size nationwide, starting and maximum salaries would have to be increased $200 and $900, respectively.

Over the past several years, the crime rate in Metropolis has climbed continuously. Until this past year, the increase in reported crimes has been close to the national average. However, the statistics released for this past year indicate an alarming jump of 9.2% in the incidence of serious crimes reported. (See Appendix B.) This figure is higher than that reported for any other city in the region, and is higher than the national average in each of the past two years for cities ranging in population size from 250,000 to over one million. Several citizens' groups have vociferously decried the "rampant crime in the streets" and are demanding restoration of "law and order" to Metropolis.

Critics of Mayor Holmes attribute the rise in serious crime to his administration's "soft" position on crime and Holmes' refusal to significantly increase the budget for the Police Department. MAPO's President, L. Hand, has made several public statements supporting this view. In particular, Hand has argued that salaries and benefits for Metropolis police officers are not large enough to attract a sufficient number of qualified personnel to give adequate protection to the citizens of Metropolis. MAPO has asserted that eighteen U.S. cities with a population greater than 250,000 offer higher starting salaries to their police officers, and sixteen of those cities have higher maximum salaries. Hand has also accused Holmes of a lack of concern about controlling

2

crime, pointing to the fact that Metropolis' $86.90 per capita expenditure for police protection is far below the national average for cities the size of Metropolis. (See Appendix C.)

The Mayor's supporters argue that the recent surge in crime is not the fault of his administration, but rather has causes that are rooted in the complex socioeconomic problems of American urban centers in general. Moreover, they assert that the 9.2% figure is misleading and does not accurately reflect the level of crime increase in Metropolis. Specifically, they argue that the reported 9.2% increase in crime is largely due to several nights of rioting in Metropolis' largest slum area during this past summer and that, excluding the data for those three days and nights, Metropolis' crime increase would have been only 4% over last year. In addition, the Mayor's supporters contend that since Metropolis' crime rate was relatively low to begin with, even a real increase of 9.2% would still leave Metropolis a relatively safe community compared to other cities in the region. Finally, they point out that Holmes was elected on a platform of fiscal responsibility and reduced tax burdens. In claiming that Holmes has a "mandate from the people" to stop the flood of tax dollars to municipal employees, they insist that the Police Department should not be the sole municipal department to be immune from the effects of the budget cutter's axe.

Discontent among MAPO members with Holmes' administration has been steadily mounting over the past year. Immediately after assuming the mayoralty, Holmes alienated many members of the force by appointing a crony, Fran Friendly, as Commissioner of Police. Friendly had no law enforcement experience whatsoever, and many police officers felt that Friendly's appointment foreshadowed an undue and dangerous politicization of the Police Department. These fears were compounded when Holmes and Friendly collaborated to propose a program of mandatory drug testing that would give Friendly wide discretion in determining when and how the testing procedures are implemented. A petition signed by 95% of the members of the force has denounced the drug testing program in its presently proposed form as a potential tool of coercion to threaten the reputation and employability of those to whom it may arbitrarily be applied.

Metropolis police officers were also outraged by Holmes' administration's position on upgrading police weaponry. Police departments in other heavy crime areas have begun to issue 9 mm semiautomatic pistols to officers, so police weaponry will be competitive with the arsenals encountered on the street. Metropolis, however, as an economy measure, has delayed implementing a program to replace the .38 revolvers that are currently issued to Metropolis police officers. This is an especially sensitive issue, because just last year one Metropolis police officer was killed in the line of duty by a suspect's semiautomatic weapon when the officer had to stop to reload his revolver. In terms of assaults against and work-related injuries or deaths of police officers, Metropolis is statistically the 10th most dangerous city in the nation for a police officer.

The release of the past year's crime statistics has combined with rumors that Holmes' administration is going to propose a 0% increase for the Police Department budget to bring matters to a head. Immediately following a news story about the rumored level-funding,

3

eighteen junior police officers announced their intention to resign from the force if salaries are not increased for the next fiscal year. The City's Budget Director, W. Hoover, responded that Holmes' administration would not change any tentative budgetary allocations under pressure, but refused to confirm the accuracy of the report on the Police Department budget. It is widely known that the Mayor expressed dismay at the magnitude of the figures compiled by Hoover's office in a recent study of the cost of modifying the salary scale, operating procedures, and/or fringe benefits for Metropolis police officers. A table of these cost figures is presented in Appendix D. The news report suggested that Holmes had refused to approve any expensive changes in pay or benefits and decided to allocate the Police Department virtually the same amount for the coming fiscal year as the Department received this year.

In a widely quoted statement, MAPO Chief Hand indicated that MAPO members would almost certainly be forced to engage in "some kind of protest activity," maybe even a strike, unless police officers' salary and benefits are increased and working conditions ameliorated. Hand reportedly said, "I want my MAPO members to be adequately compensated for undertaking the dangerous duties they perform each day, and to be permitted to effect operating procedures maximizing their safety." The Mayor's office reacted strongly to these remarks. Holmes was quoted as saying: "Continuous and uninterrupted service by the Police Department to the citizens of Metropolis is absolutely essential for the protection of the public health, safety, and welfare." The Mayor was adamant in insisting that, under state law, the police officers have no right to engage in any form of work stoppage, slowdown, or strike, and that any violation of this law would be punished to the fullest extent possible.

The Police Department had little popular support for its demands until the crime statistics for this past year were released. Now, however, as a result of articles, television reports, and editorials on crime and the problems of urban law enforcement, the perceived legitimacy of MAPO's demands has vastly increased. Two separate polls, hastily compiled in recent days, indicate that while 70% of the electorate approves of Mayor Holmes' budget cuts, only about 40% believe that Holmes' administration has been doing a good job overall. Less than 35% of those polled believe Commissioner Friendly to be doing a good job.

Mayor Holmes' term will expire in approximately fourteen months. The Mayor is eligible for and probably will seek a second term. Aware that public attention on the crime issue and open friction with the police may jeopardize the chances for reelection, the Mayor has quietly approached Hand to see what can be done about resolving problems between the City and the police force. Hand, representing MAPO, has agreed to a closed meeting with the City representatives, but once again has stressed that if something is not done to improve the lot of Metropolis police officers, a "major protest activity of some kind" might be impossible to prevent or control.

4

Metropolis Police Department

BUDGET HISTORY

The total Metropolis Police Department Budget has increased in each of the last five years:

Fiscal Year	Police Budget	% Increase Over Previous Year
−1 (this year)	$61,875,000	3%
−2 (last year)	$60,072,800	4%
−3	$57,762,300	3%
−4	$56,079,900	4%
−5	$53,923,000	7%
−6	$50,395,800	

Note: For a breakdown of budget appropriations for the past two fiscal years, see Appendix E. You should assume for purposes of this case that the current rate of inflation is 12%, and that during the past five fiscal years the inflation rate has averaged between 9% and 12%.

5

City of Metropolis Police Department

APPROPRIATION DETAIL: Fiscal Year –1

Groups and Classes	Department Total	% of Total
Personal Services		
Permanent Employment		
Emergency Employment		
Overtime		
Unemployment Compensation		
TOTAL PERSONAL SERVICES	$56,492,000	91.3%
Energy		
Light, Heat, & Power		
Auto Energy Supply		
Heating Supplies &		
Materials		
TOTAL ENERGY	1,423,000	2.3%
Contractual Services		
Communications		
Repair of Bldg. & Structure		
Repair/Service of Equipment		
Transportation of Persons		
Misc. Contractual Services		
TOTAL CONTRACTUAL SERVICES	1,485,000	2.4%
Supplies and Materials		
Food Supplies		
Household Supplies & Materials		
Medical & Dental Supplies		
Office Supplies & Materials		
Clothing Allowance		
Misc. Supplies & Materials		
TOTAL SUPPLIES & MATERIALS	1,547,000	2.5%
Current Charges		
Other Current Charges		
TOTAL CURRENT CHARGES	619,000	1.0%
Equipment		
Automotive Equipment		
Office Furniture & Equipment		
Misc. Equipment		
TOTAL EQUIPMENT	309,000	0.5%
TOTAL NON-PERSONAL SERVICES	5,383,000	8.7%
GRAND TOTAL	61,875,000	

6

Appendix A

City	Total (x 1000)	% population change over last 5 years	Population						
			Ethnic Origin		Age Groups			Median Age (years)
			% white	% non-white	% < 18 yrs.	% 18-64 yrs.	% 65+ yrs.	
Browntown	1,015	16.00	76.2	23.8	24.2	66.1	9.7	28.3
Erieville	324	17.3	67.6	32.4	24.6	61.8	13.6	31.4
Metropolis	712	13.1	73.6	26.4	31.0	62.8	6.2	27.4
Miranda City	359	8.6	81.7	18.3	25.5	62.8	11.7	28.3
Palsgraf Falls	104	0.8	66.0	34.0	15.4	73.8	10.8	29.0
Polemusburg	894	13.2	84.3	15.7	29.0	61.7	9.3	28.9
Schaeffer Heights	505	2.5	74.8	25.2	22.5	64.9	12.6	30.2

7

Appendix A (continued)

City	Population					
	Education			Economics		
	% < 5 years of school	% high school graduates	% 4+ years of college	Per capita income ($)	% of labor force unemployed	% below poverty line
Browntown	2.8	78.9	24.0	11,766	5.0	12.4
Erieville	3.9	71.6	18.7	10,627	6.9	15.0
Metropolis	3.7	76.4	21.1	12,583	6.8	8.2
Miranda City	3.2	72.7	19.2	9,430	5.7	14.7
Palsgraf Falls	1.9	86.4	52.3	12,965	6.0	21.0
Polemusburg	2.9	73.3	16.5	11,363	5.8	11.1
Schaeffer Heights	2.5	74.7	24.8	12,490	7.2	13.7

Appendix A (continued)

City	Total Crime	Crime			
		Rate per 1000 of population	Violent Crime	Property Crime	Annual Change in Total (%)
Browntown	67,893	68.70	6,250	61,643	6.7
Erieville	33,908	108.35	3,681	30,227	3.7
Metropolis	44,224	62.11	3,470	40,754	9.2
Miranda City	38,249	100.27	3,713	34,536	5.8
Palsgraf Falls	13,199	123.62	1,164	12,035	2.8
Polemusburg	82,523	92.64	7,521	75,002	5.5
Schaeffer Heights	53,234	103.76	4,252	48,982	1.7

59

Appendix B

City	Total Officers	Officers Per 1000 Population	Starting Salary (x $1000)	Maximum Salary (x $1000)	Total Expenditure for Force (x $1000)	Expenditure Per Capita ($)
Browntown	1,407	1.39	21.0	31.1	100,850	99.36
Erieville	502	1.55	23.7	31.5	48,292	149.05
Metropolis	976	1.37	22.5	29.5	61,875	86.90
Miranda City	647	1.80	21.3	27.9	43,234	120.43
Palsgraf Falls	173	1.66	29.6	46.9	9,089	87.39
Polemusburg	1,704	1.91	22.2	31.5	123,667	138.33
Schaeffer Heights	1,349	2.67	23.5	35.8	75,381	149.27
Metropolis Fire Department	654	--	23.0	30.0	--	--

Appendix B (continued)

City	Life Ins. (x salary)	Pension (% of salary x yrs)	Vacation Days (up to 5 yrs on force/ after 5th year)	Sick Leave (# of days)	Paid Holidays (# of days)	Available Cafeteria Plan Options (Off-Duty Benefits)						Type of Weapon
						Hosp.	Med.	Surg.	Dent.	Liab. Insur.	Emp'ee Asst.	
Browntown	1.5	1.75	7/15	11	8	x	x	x	x	Legal repr.	Stress mgnt.	9 mm
Erieville	1.5	2.25	11/16	15	10	--	--	--	--	--	--	.38
Metropolis	1.0	2.00	10/15	10	7	x	x	x	x	--	--	.38
Miranda City	2.0	2.25	14/20	10	10	x	x	x	x	Legal repr.	Stress mgnt.	.38
Palsgraf Falls	2.0	2.00	15/21	20	10	x	x	x	x	--	--	.38
Polemus- burg	1.5	2.25	12/17	15	8	--	--	--	x	--	--	9 mm
Schaeffer Heights	1.0	2.00	11/17	12	9	--	--	--	--	--	--	9 mm
Metropolis Fire Dept.	1.0	2.00	12/17	15	7	x	x	x	x	--	Stress mgnt.	--

Appendix C

Popu-lation Group	Mean # of Officers	Per 1000 Pop.	Mean Starting Salary ($)	Mean Maximum Salary ($)	Total Person-nel Expense	Salary & Wages	Soc. Sec. & Retire-ment	Health, Hosp., Dis., & Life Ins.	Total Capital Outlay	Other	Total Police Expense
							($ Per Capita)				
Over 1,000,000	7,017	3.95	25,312	32,536	196.57	134.06	50.02	12.48	1.59	16.98	213.56
500,000-1,000,000	1,949	2.89	22,715	30,582	124.17	93.75	24.91	5.50	1.44	21.31	145.49
250,000-499,999	880	2.75	21,697	28,842	103.44	80.87	15.31	7.25	2.69	17.28	120.73
100,000-249,999	329	2.44	22,583	28,979	92.08	72.97	13.58	5.53	2.72	14.83	106.92
50,000-99,999	147	2.28	22,425	28,855	90.62	70.69	13.47	6.45	3.47	13.23	103.85
25,000-49,999	77	2.31	21,342	27,871	80.71	64.45	11.17	5.09	3.36	14.83	99.55
10,000-24,999	35	2.31	19,612	25,318	76.16	61.52	9.68	4.95	7.48	13.72	89.88

Source: *Municipal Year Book for Fiscal Year 1*

12

Appendix D

Cost Increases for Metropolis Police Department

<u>Issue</u>	<u>Annual Cost*</u>
1. Starting Salary**	$88,000 for *each* $100 increase
2. Maximum Salary**	$110,000 for *each* $100 increase
3. Vacation Days	
Up to 5 years tenure	$112,000 for *each* additional day
Over 5 years tenure	$144,000 for *each* additional day
4. Sick Leave	$280,000 for *each* additional day
5. Holidays	$240,000 for *each* additional day
6. Life Insurance	$120,000 for *each* 0.5 increase in formula
7. Pension	$480,000 for *each* 0.25% increase in formula
8. Cafeteria Plan Options (Off-duty Benefits)	
Liability Insurance:	
Legal Representation	$128,000 (level 1)
PLUS Personal Insurance	$240,000 (level 2)
Employee Assistance:	
Stress Counseling	$240,000 (level 1)
PLUS Substance Abuse Counseling	$320,000 (level 2)
PLUS Fitness Counseling	$400,000 (level 3)
9. Weaponry	$100,000 for *each* 25% of the force to convert to 9 mm semiautomatic pistols (including replacement costs for holsters and ammunition)

APPENDIX E

City of Metropolis

*All cost figures presented assume implementation of the proposed change for the entire force or for the entire portion of the force eligible to receive such benefits.

**Salary increase cost figures reflect increases in budget items contingent upon salary (e.g., overtime pay, pension fund contributions, and life insurance premiums), as well as the actual base cost of additional salary payments. Thus, while an annual pay increase of $100 for all 976 officers would involve an actual salary expenditure increase of $97,600, the total cost to Metropolis would be $198,000.

13

BUDGET SUMMARY

Municipal Dept.	Fiscal Year (FY) –2 Appropriation ($)	Mayor's Rec. % Increase	Mayor's FY –1 Recommended Appropriation ($)	Actual FY –1 Appropriation ($)	Actual % Increase
Admin. Services	47,486,800	6.0	50,340,000	50,336,000	6.0
Auditing	1,426,300	5.0	1,497,600	1,497,600	5.0
City Clerk	429,700	6.5	457,600	457,600	6.5
City Council	5,859,200	6.5	6,240,000	6,240,000	6.5
Courts/ Corrections	1,938,600	18.6	2,300,000	1,996,800	3.0
Education	59,763,400	6.5	63,648,000	63,648,000	6.5
Fair Housing	200,000	4.0	208,000	208,000	4.0
Fire	41,200,000	4.0	42,848,000	42,848,000	4.0
Health/Hospitals	87,368,800	7.0	93,500,000	95,232,000	9.0
Law	3,006,700	1.1	3,040,000	3,036,800	1.0
Libraries	5,150,500	5.0	5,408,000	5,408,000	5.0
Mayor's Office	1,015,600	6.5	1,081,600	1,081,600	6.5
Parks/Recreation	9,600,000	4.2	10,000,000	9,984,000	4.0
Police	60,072,800	3.0	61,875,000	61,875,000	3.0
Public Works	29,547,700	7.0	31,616,000	31,616,000	7.0
Rent Control	680,000	4.4	710,000	707,200	4.0
Traffic/Parking	11,308,700	3.0	11,648,000	11,648,000	3.0
Workers' Comp.	2,258,300	6.3	2,400,000	2,371,200	5.0
Other	21,751,000	--	27,808,200*	25,808,200	--
Totals	**390,064,100**	**6.8**	**416,626,000**	**416,000,000**	**6.7**

*This recommendation included $2,000,000 for proposed renovations to four Department of Public Works maintenance garages. The Mayor and City Council agreed to delete this request from the final budget appropriation.

14

MAPO
CITY OF METROPOLIS NEGOTIATION

Confidential Information for City of Metropolis Representatives

In these discussions you represent the City of Metropolis and work for Mayor Holmes' administration. As members of the negotiating team, you have full authority to make agreements in the Mayor's name and on behalf of the Mayor (subject only to the restrictions outlined in the following instructions).

The Mayor is deeply perturbed by the recent surge in crime and, even more, by his recent plunge in popularity with the electorate. Holmes has told you, members of the inner circle, that the problems with the Police Department should be resolved quickly and quietly. Political opponents predicted that lack of funding to the Department would cause problems, and Holmes wants to avoid an alliance between MAPO, other municipal workers' organizations, and political adversaries. On the other hand, the hard reality is that the fiscal picture for the city is, indeed, bleak, and that certain influential groups view almost any gesture of support for the police to be a hostile act. Thus, on balance, Holmes demands that an understanding be reached with MAPO without loss of face or at too great expense.

Statements attributed to officials of Holmes' administration relating to the tight fiscal situation are quite true, at least in the sense that legitimate demands on Metropolis' resources far exceed existing and projected revenues. Significant tax increases would be political suicide, and even a modest tax hike would probably make Holmes a one-term Mayor. Nevertheless, there does exist a certain flexibility in the budget-making process, which permits increases in allocations to certain departments even if other departments must face budget cuts. The current draft of the Mayor's Fiscal Year 0 budget recommendations is attached. After lengthy discussions with Hoover and other budget officers, Holmes has concluded that the Police Department budget may be increased by 5% ($3.09 million) without placing much of a strain on other departments. The Mayor would be quite satisfied with a settlement in the area of 5%, but would be delighted if a lesser figure could be agreed upon. There are many, many deserving priorities that the Mayor will not be able to fund this year; any money saved on the police budget will be well spent somewhere else. An increase of 8% ($4.95 million) is possible, but would require significant juggling of the allocations to other portions of the municipal budget. Holmes has made it clear that any increase in the 10% range should be accepted only if necessary to avoid a major strike by MAPO. Any increase above 10% would require the Mayor's personal approval.

In addition to the generally tight financial situation, Holmes' desire for fiscal restraint in departmental budgets reflects a strong belief that the municipal budget should incorporate a "discretionary fund" for emergencies. Such a fund would be available to supplement any department's budget in the event of unexpected and unavoidable unbudgeted expenses. Past budgets have had no such reserve, often resulting in operating deficits. Such a fund might be used, for example, to pay the cost of water acquisition and conservation measures in cases of drought such as occurred during the summer a year ago, to offset the effects of a strike by hospital nurses, to defend against a major lawsuit against the police department, or to hire temporary officers to deal with a summer riot. Such unforeseen emergencies have arisen with regularity, and the Mayor considers such a fund to be a basic requirement of sound fiscal policy that would benefit all city employees, including the police. Holmes plans to finance the discretionary fund by setting aside 3% of the total city budget. Although this will mean that many departments will not get the budget increase they expect or desire, they should be able to access the discretionary fund in the event a legitimate need arose.

The Mayor's political analysts believe that Proposition 6 is likely to be approved in the upcoming referendum, but they expect the vote to be much closer than recent polls have indicated. While you may argue that the Administration feels constrained by the 6% figure, you would have to concede that Proposition 6 has no binding force until passed (i.e., there is no legal impediment to increasing the Police Department budget for Fiscal Year 0 more than 6%). Moreover, the Mayor wishes to keep his administration's budgetary options open. Indeed, Holmes has said flatly that his administration will not commit to limiting departmental budget increases to 6% or less in anticipation of Proposition 6 coming into force. Ever since proponents of Proposition 6 got it on the ballot last year, the Mayor has resisted pressure to declare voluntary compliance with the measure, insisting on case-by-case analysis of departmental needs. While Holmes would in fact like to keep all departmental budget increases to less than 6%, the Mayor also anticipates that there may be areas where a greater increase seems necessary (particularly in the smaller departments desperately in need of new equipment).

While Proposition 6 may have no direct impact on the overall Police Department budget increase, it will clearly be central to any discussion about the duration of a City-Police agreement. Holmes adamantly does not want to be placed in the position of having to renegotiate the agreement in the hectic months prior to the mayoral election. A one-year agreement, which would expire just two months before the election, is thus unacceptable. Any period less than a year seems simply too short. As long as the agreement lapses after the election, however, the Mayor has no particular preference as to duration. Nationwide, there is a trend toward longer term, multiple-year contracts, but this is usually on the initiative of the police department, on terms quite favorable to them, and as a product of some sort of collective bargaining process. You should bear in mind that the longer the agreement lasts, the greater the benefits MAPO will demand. While a "favorable" agreement with a long term (i.e., longer than two years) may seem beneficial, you should recognize that there can be no real guarantee that MAPO will not breach the agreement, threaten another illegal strike, or demand greater benefits prior to the expiration of the agreement. For this reason the Mayor is unwilling to trade off greater concessions on benefits for a long duration. You may consider any reasonable built-in

　　　　　　2

escalator clauses to a longer-term agreement, but in general Holmes would prefer flexibility in the budgeting process and is wary of committing to future budget increases for which funds may simply not be available.

It is essential that, in discussing the various issues with MAPO, you keep a careful tally of any concessions made and of the total cost incurred. Making piecemeal concessions can rapidly lead to a huge budget increase, unless negotiators keep a running total of the costs of items tentatively discussed and resolved. For many of the issues MAPO is likely to bring up, Holmes must consider the impact of a concession on other departmental budgets as well as the cost for the police. Whenever one set of municipal employees gets an increase in some kind of benefit, all the other municipal departments are quick to demand identical treatment. Although MAPO representatives may cogently argue that the dangers inherent in law enforcement warrant benefits in excess of those received by teachers or hospital workers, you should stress the impossibility of persuading other departments that their budgets should be cut to finance increases in all of the police's fringe benefits.

For the above reasons, Holmes feels quite strongly that there should be few, if any, changes in the police fringe benefits, which are currently uniform for all municipal employees (including police officers, fire fighters, hospital workers, teachers, and department of public works and City Hall employees). These uniform benefits are life insurance, cafeteria plan benefits, pensions, and paid holidays. Of these, it is only official holidays that would clearly require identical benefits to be extended to all municipal employees. Therefore, it would be highly desirable to keep Metropolis employees' holidays to the current level of seven (which includes New Year's, Easter, Memorial Day, Independence Day, Labor Day, Thanksgiving, and Christmas). Any change from the status quo would surely invite all other municipal employees to demand equal treatment. Although not a dire consequence in and of itself, this might precipitate the far graver specter of new contract talks on all issues with other departments.

In the area of cafeteria plan benefits and life insurance, the ideal would be to keep these items at current levels, uniform for all departments. The Mayor recognizes that the job of law enforcement in Metropolis is far more dangerous than teaching or collecting garbage, and you should anticipate MAPO arguing strenuously that its members deserve benefits far exceeding those given to other municipal employees. But the Mayor feels that existing cafeteria plan options are adequate, because they offer off-duty hospital, medical, surgical, and dental plans to supplement the provision of on-duty, work-related emergency surgical and dental work, which is the major legitimate concern of law enforcement officers. The Mayor would prefer not to indemnify individual police officers through liability insurance, since such indemnity might create a conflict of interest if the City wanted claims against a police officer tried separately from claims against the City. The Metropolis Fire Department has recently established a stress management employee assistance program, and the police may want a comparable program to help them cope with the stresses and demands of the job. If maintaining the status quo with regard to life insurance and cafeteria plan options seems impossible, you are authorized to make whatever reasonable concessions appear necessary in these two issues, but you should try to keep any such increases to a minimum. It may be useful to note that the Fire Department (doing

3

statistically more dangerous work) still has the uniform Metropolis employee life insurance schedule, no liability insurance option, and only the minimum level of employee assistance.

The last of the uniform fringe benefits, pensions, is the one that most troubles Mayor Holmes. The current pension program in the Department pays officers an annual pension of 2% of their highest base salary times the total number of years they were on the force. Even small increases in the pension formula are enormously expensive, and will be a tremendous burden to this and all subsequent administrations. Beyond the dollar cost of a pension formula change for the Police Department, once again, the city will have to face demands for similar pension increases by all other groups of municipal workers. In these future negotiations it will be difficult to convince representatives of other municipal employees that there is any justification whatsoever for differential pension formulae for the various groups of municipal workers. (Note: Because differential salaries may be justified far more easily than differential pension formulae, the Mayor would prefer to increase a police officer's starting salary by $800 than to increase the pension formula by .25%, even though the present cost of the former is greater.) The Mayor has indicated that every effort should be made to retain the present 2.0% pension formula; Holmes could, however, live with a 2.25% formula, if it appeared absolutely necessary to reach agreement with MAPO. Any agreement providing for an increase above 2.25% would require the Mayor's personal approval.

As has already been intimated in the discussion above, Holmes feels considerably less constrained about granting salary hikes than about making concessions in other areas. Notwithstanding the rhetoric concerning lack of funds for any salary increases, Holmes has anticipated that a pay hike would have to be made to both Fire Department and Police Department personnel. In fact, although it has been a closely guarded secret, Holmes and Hoover were prepared to grant a 5% across-the-board salary increase to all municipal workers for the present fiscal year (−1), after such an increase was granted to teachers, but other departments did not press too hard for it. With the current popular outcry against increasing crime and growing sympathy for police officers, the Mayor feels it would be politically advantageous to increase salaries as evidence of his dedication to high quality law enforcement in Metropolis. The Mayor feels that the police deserve at least parity with firemen's wages (which for next year, although not yet publicly disclosed, are tentatively set respectively at $700 and $900 above Police Department starting and maximum salaries for this year). Holmes would not be upset with a 5% increase in both starting and maximum salaries, amounting to $1100 and $1500, respectively (although, as with all these issues, he would be delighted with lesser increases). If pushed, you may agree to a starting salary increase of up to $1600, and a maximum salary increase of up to $2000, which would represent more than a 7% increase in officers' salary. These figures, however, are the absolute maximum that you have authority to agree to without the Mayor's personal approval, and the 7% figure should be used only if it appears absolutely necessary to achieve a settlement.

On the issues of vacation time and sick leave, Mayor Holmes feels that the present 10/15 vacation schedule and 10 sick days are adequate for the needs of MAPO members. Prior to this fiscal year, these regimes were uniform for all municipal employees in Metropolis. It is only the

4

Fire Department that currently deviates from the old system. The reason that Holmes agreed to increase vacation and sick leave for fire fighters was that Fire Department officials agreed to forego a pay increase and acquiesce to certain cuts in service in return for these two concessions. With the service cuts, the Fire Department was quite fully staffed, therefore the increase in time off for firemen involved no additional expense for the city. This is clearly not true for the Police Department. Suffering from a chronic shortage of officers (partly due to budgetary limitations), the Police Department currently is barely staffed at adequate levels. Any additional time off would necessitate costly overtime coverage by existing officers or the addition of new officers to the force, neither of which the Department can afford. Therefore, every effort should be made to retain the present vacation and sick leave schedule. Specifically, the Mayor feels that any agreement to allow a total of more than three additional days off in these two areas combined should be made only subject to the Mayor's personal approval. (Count each additional vacation day for both tenure groups as one additional day and each additional day for only one tenure group as a one-half day increase; for example, a 12/17, an 11/18, or a 10/19 day vacation schedule would be a 2-day increase, as would an 11/16 vacation schedule plus one additional sick day).

MAPO spokespersons have vociferously complained about the inadequacy of the weapons issued by the Police Department as compared to the powerful semiautomatic weapons encountered on the street. Since Mayor Holmes is sincerely concerned about the recent surge in crime (and, more importantly, the public's criticism of the Holmes administration's law enforcement policies), the Mayor would like to assuage MAPO's concerns for the safety of Metropolis police officers. In truth, though, the Mayor is somewhat skeptical of claims that the streets are so dangerous that every police officer needs to trade in a revolver for a semiautomatic pistol. Holmes regrets the loss of the police officer who was killed in the line of duty, but the Mayor believes that the unfortunate incident was an anomaly that does not warrant purchasing all new guns, holsters, and ammunition for every member of the police force, unless MAPO seems to require it for reaching a settlement. While this is one of the few areas where cost really is not a significant concern, the Mayor is worried that a sudden, full conversion of Police Department weaponry from .38 revolvers to 9 mm semiautomatic pistols will be seen as an admission that inattention on the part of Holmes and Friendly contributed in some way to the death of the police officer. Thus, "upgrading" some weaponry can be rationalized based on the new crime statistics, but a major change in the arsenal should be avoided without first obtaining the Mayor's personal approval.

Commissioner Friendly has been another bone of contention with MAPO. This issue is far more complex than meets the eye. On the one hand, Friendly has become a political liability to the Mayor, who would welcome an opportunity to have Friendly depart from the Holmes administration. On the other hand, it would not behoove Holmes to acquire a reputation for dumping political allies (and former friends) as soon as an unfavorable public opinion poll is released. Therefore, this issue needs to be treated with great delicacy. Ideally, you should only "acquiesce" to dumping Friendly after suitable pressure is exerted by MAPO, so that it does not appear that Holmes is anxious to get rid of the Commissioner. The Mayor will be delighted if you can get agreement to throw out the Police Commissioner and have it received as a major

5

concession on the part of Holmes.

It is quite likely that MAPO representatives will demand that the drug testing proposal be withdrawn or restructured to eliminate the exercise of discretion in implementation procedures. Mayor Holmes views the drug testing program as one of the Administration's most significant achievements. The Mayor is adamant that the program be implemented. However, if the discretionary implementation issue is a major impediment to concluding a successful agreement, the Mayor would be willing to allow some police input in crafting prescribed implementation procedures, to assuage fears of arbitrariness and coercion. Allowing the police actually to set implementation policy, or to severely curtail all discretion on the part of the Mayor and the Commissioner in implementing the drug testing program, would require Holmes' personal approval, and would be only marginally preferable to abandoning the proposal entirely.

To sum up, this memorandum outlines the goals of the Holmes administration in the upcoming discussions with MAPO. Mayor Holmes requires that you balance the aspirations of avoiding a strike and improving the morale and effectiveness of the police force with efforts to limit budget increases, minimize the setting of precedents for other municipal departments, and protect Holmes' political integrity. While it is acceptable for you to agree to the maximum permitted increase in one or several of the areas for discussion, Holmes would be extremely displeased if you agreed to the limit on virtually all of the issues in dispute, and in no event may you exceed the Mayor's maximum 10% budget increase guideline without obtaining Holmes' personal approval. The Mayor wants to make peace with MAPO, but believes that the Mayor's primary duty is to the electorate at large, which has clearly articulated its desire for fiscal restraint. Even though breaking off negotiations with no agreement may well result in some kind of strike (which would inevitably wreak havoc in Metropolis), no agreement is clearly preferable to giving in to unreasonable demands by MAPO.

Municipal Department	% Increase Over FY −1	FY 0 Mayor's Plan**	Possible % Increase Over FY −1
Administrative Services			5.0
Auditing	4.0	$ 1,557,500	
City Clerk	2.0	446,800	
City Council	6.0	6,614,400	
Courts/ Corrections			3.0
Education			6.0
Fair Housing	2.0	212,200	
Fire			5.0
Health/Hospitals			6.0
Law	0.0	3,036,800	
Libraries	1.0	5,462,100	
Mayor's Office	6.0	1,146,500	
Parks/Recreation	1.0	10,038,800	
Police			5.0
Public Works			3.0
Rent Control	2.0	721,300	
Traffic/Parking	-2.0	11,415,000	
Worker's Compensation	2.0	2,418,600	
Other			
Discretionary Fund (3% of total annual budget)		13,104,000	
Target Recommendation	5.0	436,800,000	
Revenue Projection For Fiscal Year 1990		436,800,000	

*Mayor Holmes is committed to making certain budget recommendations for twelve city departments. The Mayor has also determined approximate percentage increases for the budgets of the remaining departments. These figures are not final, however, and may well be affected by these discussions with MAPO.

**These departmental figures assume the existence of the Mayor's proposed discretionary fund.

MAPO-City of Metropolis Negotiation
CITY REPRESENTATIVES' REPORT FORM

Issue	Change Agreed To	Total Cost of Item
1. Starting Salary	$_____ increase	$_____
2. Maximum Salary	$_____ increase	$_____
3. Vacation Days -Up to 5 years tenure:	_____ additional day(s)	$_____
-Over 5 years tenure:	_____ additional day(s)	$_____
4. Sick Leave	_____ additional day(s)	$_____
5. Holidays	_____ additional day(s)	$_____
6. Life Insurance	Increase of _____% x salary	$_____
7. Pension	Increase of _____% x salary	$_____
8. Cafeteria Plan Options Liability Insurance (Circle one) none level 1 level 2		$_____
Employee Assistance (Circle one) none level 1 level 2 level 3		$_____
9. Weaponry	_____% of force converted to 9 mm semiautomatic pistols	$_____
Total Cost of Items 1-9*		$_____
10. Total Police Budget	_____% increase	$_____
11. Commissioner Friendly	In / Out	
12. Drug Testing Proposal (Circle one or more)	No Change Withdrawn Police Input on Implementation	
	Police Determine Implementation Procedures Other (specify)	
13. Duration of Agreement	_____	
14. Other terms	_____	

_____ (Continue on back)

*NOTE: If there is a negotiated settlement of the total police department budget increase, it need not be identical to the total cost of items 1-9, although obviously it should be no less than that total. Any excess budgetary increase above the cost of the individual items agreed to will go to the multitude of areas not covered in these discussions (e.g., new equipment, training, overhead expense, overtime expense, additional officers, etc.)

8

MAPO
CITY OF METROPOLIS NEGOTIATION

Confidential Information for MAPO Representatives

In these discussions you represent the Metropolis Association of Police Officers (MAPO). MAPO is an organization that is far less monolithic and unified than both the public at large and the Mayor's Office seem to believe. Although virtually all members of the force are card-carrying members of MAPO, only several dozen are activists who recognize the power MAPO could exercise as bargaining agent for all police personnel. It is imperative for the future growth and power of MAPO that its members view these discussions as being "successful."

While the ultimate weapon available to MAPO in these discussions is some kind of job action or strike, the state law is absolutely clear that any form of slowdown, work stoppage, or strike is illegal. Even an undeclared "sickout" or "blue flu" would be a clear attempt to circumvent the law and would undoubtedly trigger vigorous prosecution by the Holmes administration. The fate of striking air-traffic controllers is bound to loom large in the minds of MAPO members, and it seems evident that a majority of police officers would refuse to participate in any form of strike unless conditions deteriorate much further. In addition to being extremely divisive within MAPO, any kind of work stoppage, slowdown, or strike would also endanger both the public and its confidence in and support for the police force. Thus you should use the threat of a strike to extract every possible concession from the Administration, but should avoid at almost any cost actually having to resort to one.

You understand the dilemma that Mayor Holmes faces with regard to budget increases, but MAPO members simply do not accept broad statements that there are no funds available for increased police protection. Even in a tight fiscal situation, the municipal budget at this stage should still be highly manipulable. You are certain that the Mayor's office has a draft budget prepared, although many of the figures in it will still be very "soft." You should stress that adequate police protection is so vital to the community that a police budget increase is essential, even if it means budget cuts for other municipal departments. MAPO members seemed to feel strongly at the last meeting that in these inflationary times any increase of less than 8% in the total Police Department budget would be a significant decrease in real terms in the resources available for law enforcement. An increase in real terms (i.e., above the current inflation rate of 12%) would clearly be desirable if it is obtainable; every effort must be made to get the representatives of Mayor Holmes' administration to agree to at least an 8% overall increase (amounting to a total police budget increase of $4.95 million). If the Holmes administration refuses to go above a 5% increase ($3.09 million), the minimum demands of MAPO can just barely be met; any lesser increase is simply unacceptable.

With all the talk about Proposition 6 and the upcoming referendum, it is possible that the Holmes administration will argue that it cannot increase the police budget by more than 6%. This is nonsense. Proposition 6 has absolutely no binding force until it is passed. There is no legal problem with increasing the Police Department budget for Fiscal Year 0 in excess of 6%, and the Holmes administration has not selected any particular figure as a maximum for departmental budget increases. Any use of the 6% figure in this negotiation is likely to be nothing more than an attempt to rationalize stonewalling. Claims of a 6% constraint would be credible only if the Holmes administration publicly announced its intention to keep all departmental budget increases to a maximum of 6%. This of course is something that Holmes has repeatedly refused to do, despite considerable pressure from Proposition 6 supporters.

While Proposition 6 should have no impact whatsoever on limiting the current Police Department budget increase, it will clearly be central to the discussion of the duration of any Police-City agreement. In the event that Proposition 6 is passed, MAPO's interest is to insure that the Police Department's pre-implementation budget is as large as possible. Certainly MAPO members are unwilling to forego the increased budget allocation they need now in return for promises of greater benefits in the future, especially since the needs of the Department are likely to grow faster than the City's resources. MAPO has a great deal of leverage in negotiations with the Holmes administration, so a short duration for this agreement seems advantageous to MAPO. If the agreement were to last one year, it would expire shortly before the next mayoral election, which would be ideal for exerting pressure on the administration. Should the Holmes administration insist on a longer-term agreement, you will have to demand greater benefits that take inflation into account. You may consider any reasonable built-in escalation clauses to a longer-term agreement, but bear in mind that the Proposition 6 maximum of 6% will inevitably become a target figure for all departmental increases (as well as a limit), and any agreement would be abrogated by this or a subsequent administration if the City simply did not have the resources to meet its commitments.

Central to MAPO's demands is an increase in the pay received by Metropolis police personnel. You are aware of statements by Hoover that there may be no funds available for any salary increase, but you strongly suspect that such statements were made in anticipation of these discussions. The two components of the salary issue, starting salary and maximum salary, are separable and may be negotiated separately if you so desire. One of your basic goals as a MAPO negotiator should be to ascertain just how far salaries can be pushed up, and then to obtain the City's agreement to raise salaries that maximum possible amount. Of the two base-salary issues, a significant maximum salary increase is understandably far more important to MAPO's membership. Despite the rhetoric about the difficulty of attracting qualified new recruits, the hard reality of the situation is that Department officials have had to restrict the number of new officers in order to stay within budget. As a result, MAPO's current members would be satisfied with only a modest increase in starting salaries (although less than an $800 increase would be

2

unpalatable for symbolic reasons -- MAPO members believe they deserve a starting salary that is at least marginally higher than that received by fire fighters).

MAPO's highest priority is achieving a significant increase in officers' maximum salary. MAPO fears that senior officers will be forced to leave the department if there is not a wider gap between starting and maximum salaries. Promotion up the ranks must carry with it remunerative benefits as well as increased status and fringe benefits. In the current (−1) fiscal year, teachers in Metropolis received a 5% across-the-board salary hike, while police officers and fire department personnel had no increase. It is absolutely imperative that police officers get at least this 5% increase in maximum salary (amounting to approximately $1500) for the next fiscal year. Ideally, MAPO members would like an increase equal to the inflation rate of 12% (amounting to a $3500 hike), or even more, but it seems improbable that the austerity-minded Holmes would agree to such a jump.

In the area of "fringe benefits," MAPO's membership is acutely aware that Metropolis compares unfavorably with the other cities in the region. The job of law enforcement is more dangerous in Metropolis than in any of these other cities, and it seems only equitable that its police officers receive benefits to compensate them for the additional risk and constant tension while on duty. The issues, in order of priority for MAPO members, are: pensions, vacation, health insurance, life insurance, holidays, and sick leave. In general, while concessions by the Holmes administration in each of these areas are highly valued by MAPO, salary increases are still preferred over large increases in fringe benefits. You should also be aware that negotiating increases in pensions, health insurance, life insurance, and holidays is likely to be difficult, since these benefits are currently uniform for all municipal employees (including police officers, fire fighters, teachers, hospital workers, public works personnel, and City Hall employees).

The current pension program in the Department pays officers an annual pension of 2% of their highest base salary times the total number of years they were on the force. Unionized employees in the private sector frequently receive contracts using a 3% figure for this calculation. MAPO's view is that police officers deserve at least the 2.25% figure used by several other police departments in the region. Although there was no formal vote taken, the consensus at the last MAPO membership meeting seemed to be that this 0.25% increase is the minimum amount that would be acceptable to MAPO members.

The present vacation program annually credits 10 days paid vacation to each officer with under 5 years of service; each officer with longer tenure on the force receives 15 days (this program is referred to as a 10/15 vacation program). The fire department operates on a 12/17 vacation program, and MAPO members feel they deserve at least equal treatment. If it becomes necessary to choose between additional vacation time for junior officers as opposed to additional days for those with greater than 5 years tenure, it would be preferable to give senior officers the additional time.

The Department currently allows 10 paid sick days to members of the force. Although this number is generally viewed as adequate to cover actual illnesses, any additional sick days would

3

be considered equivalent to additional vacation days (because officers inevitably take advantage of all of the non-accruable sick days allotted to them). Thus, while there is no particular necessity to increase the amount of sick leave, it is a means of increasing the number of paid days off that MAPO members will receive (which is, of course, highly valued by the membership).

Official holidays for the force include New Year's Day, Easter, Memorial Day, Independence Day, Labor Day, Thanksgiving, and Christmas. The Department has a relatively high percentage of African-American and Jewish officers among its members. The current holiday schedule does not include Martin Luther King, Jr. Day or any of the Jewish holidays. If the Administration could be convinced of the political benefit of declaring holidays on Martin Luther King, Jr. Day and Yom Kippur, MAPO would gain favor with these two important minority groups, and other officers would be able to reap the benefits of additional full days of overtime pay (since, even on an official holiday, a large number of officers must still be on duty). Alternatively, or in conjunction with the above, MAPO might try to have Washington's and/or Lincoln's Birthday declared a holiday for the Department. Washington's Birthday is a holiday for state, but not municipal, employees.

With the threat of personal liability for actions taken in the course of police work and with the stresses that police work place on an officer's physical and mental well-being, it would be a great coup if MAPO could secure expanded options under the municipal employees' cafeteria plan. The current plan offers off-duty health, medical, surgical, and dental benefits. Work-related emergency surgical and dental work is provided by the Police Department. The first level of liability insurance would provide an officer with legal representation in the event that he or she were sued personally. The second level would protect the officer's personal assets, in addition to providing legal representation. Many police departments around the country have begun to offer employee assistance programs to help officers cope with the rigors and demands of police work. The first level of employee assistance would provide stress management counseling. This would not only help many officers' on-the-job performance, but might also reduce the incidence of domestic problems, which are prevalent among families of police officers. The second level of employee assistance would provide substance abuse counseling in addition to stress management counseling. Alcohol abuse may result if an officer habitually turns to alcohol as a means of letting off steam after a stressful day's work. The third level of employee assistance adds fitness counseling to the package. This would entail diagnostic and follow-up fitness evaluations and the purchase of equipment for a supervised fitness regimen. This would improve the officers' overall health and well-being, would aid in stress management, would improve the officers' job performance, and would decrease the risk of liability and inefficiency that the City fears in the specter of the overweight police officer who has a heart attack while attempting to chase a suspect. If this third level of employee assistance is provided, however, MAPO employees would prefer that the workout time be counted as on-duty time. Arguments about the dangers of police work may be made for increasing life insurance coverage, although MAPO members would far prefer expanded cafeteria plan options over large increases in life insurance.

The major issues relating to the operation of the Police Department are the type of weapons

4

issued, Commissioner Friendly, and the proposed drug testing program. Highly emotional responses on all of these issues can be readily evoked from most members of the force. The .38 revolvers which the Department currently issues to its officers must be reloaded every six shots, while 9 mm. semiautomatic pistols can fire fifteen rounds without reloading and can be fired more quickly. Last year, a police officer was killed by a suspect's semiautomatic pistol; the officer had stopped to reload his revolver at the time. MAPO members feel strongly that this tragic incident would not have occurred if the Holmes administration had followed the lead of other crime-plagued cities and had upgraded the police-issue arsenal to 9 mm semiautomatic pistols.

Commissioner Friendly is widely seen as a political crony of the Mayor's, lacking the leadership necessary to maintain morale in the force in these difficult times. Even though most MAPO members would concede that Friendly is at least marginally competent, it seems that they would prefer to have a hard-core "law enforcement type" as Commissioner. Realistically, it is unlikely that Holmes would be willing to dump a close personal friend, but it might prove useful to use the well-known dissatisfaction with Friendly to extract other, more valuable concessions from the Administration.

The drug testing proposal has tremendously irritated members of the force. Although most police officers admit the vital importance of a drug-free police force, MAPO fears the abuse of the wide discretion to implement the program, which is left in the hands of the Mayor and the Commissioner. Specifically, MAPO fears that only the junior officers, or those who disagree with certain departmental policies or procedures, will be subjected to the drug testing. Furthermore, MAPO fears the very act of singling out an officer for a drug test may be detrimental to his or her career advancement, so the threat of the test itself may exert a subtle form of coercion among members of the force. On the other hand, many MAPO members are adamant that a *mandatory* drug testing program would call their integrity as a force into question, and violate their dignity. This is an extremely volatile issue. The best resolution of it, from MAPO's perspective, would be the withdrawal of the drug testing proposal. Barring that, MAPO should get an agreement that allows the police to set the implementation procedures, or at least one that guarantees police input into the setting of implementation procedures.

MAPO considers the central issues for discussion to be maximum salary, pensions, weaponry, starting salary, drug testing, vacations, expanded cafeteria plan options, life insurance, Commissioner Friendly, holidays, and sick leave, roughly in that order of priority. For an agreement to be acceptable, MAPO members seem to feel it should provide for an increase of at least $800 in starting salaries and $1500 in maximum salaries, 9 mm semiautomatic pistols for at least 75% of the force, and at least a 2.25% pension formula. It is clear that MAPO will refuse even to consider any agreement in which the Holmes administration promises only to remove Friendly, withdraw the drug testing proposal, and/or change the type of weapons issued.

5

MAPO-City of Metropolis Negotiation
MAPO REPRESENTATIVES' REPORT FORM

Issue	Change Agreed To	Total Cost of Item
1. Starting Salary	$_____increase	$_____
2. Maximum Salary	$_____increase	$_____
3. Vacation Days		
-Up to 5 years tenure:	_____ additional day(s)	$_____
-Over 5 years tenure:	_____ additional day(s)	$_____
4. Sick Leave	_____ additional day(s)	$_____
5. Holidays	_____ additional day(s)	$_____
6. Life Insurance	Increase of _____% x salary	$_____
7. Pension	Increase of _____% x salary	$_____
8. Cafeteria Plan Options		
Liability Insurance (Circle one)	none level 1 level 2	$_____
Employee Assistance (Circle one)	none level 1 level 2 level 3	$_____
9. Weaponry	_____% of force converted to 9 mm semiautomatic pistols	$_____

Total Cost of Items 1-9* $_____

10. Total Police Budget	_____% increase	$_____
11. Commissioner Friendly	In / Out	
12. Drug Testing Proposal (Circle one or more)	No Change Withdrawn Police Input on Implementation	
	Police Determine Implementation Procedures Other (specify)	

13. Duration of Agreement _____

14. Other terms _____

_____ (Continue on back)

---

*NOTE: If there is a negotiated settlement of the total police department budget increase, it need not be identical to the total cost of items 1-9, although obviously it should be no less than that total. Any excess budgetary increase above the cost of the individual items agreed to will go to the multitude of areas not covered in these discussions (e.g., new equipment, training, overhead expense, overtime expense, additional officers, etc.)

6

DEC v. RIVERSIDE

General Information

The trial date is only three days away, but Riverside Lumber's sludge continues to flow into the Blue River. Deborah Oyer, president of Riverside, knows she might lose control of the issue, and perhaps even her company unless she reaches an agreement with the Department of Environmental Conservation (DEC) on the appropriate disposal of Riverside's effluent. Oyer does not want Riverside's future to be decided by "those dreadful lawyers in a courtroom." She hopes that today's meeting with Bill Fleming of DEC might resolve the problem.

Riverside, a wholly owned subsidiary of a multinational conglomerate, is a medium-sized pulp manufacturer in Forks, Washington. At one time, Riverside produced a wide variety of forest products, but now it specializes in pulp production. Forks, a small, one-industry town, is located on the Blue River between the Pacific Ocean and the pristine Olympic National Park. Riverside's trouble with DEC began three years earlier when the fishing industry in Washington State voiced concern over the declining salmon catch. Fishery authorities hypothesized that the problem lay in the riverbeds; spawning, they asserted, was becoming increasingly laborious because of the high pollution levels in several rivers, including the Blue. DEC, long at loggerheads with the lumber industry over pollution in the Pacific Northwest, was quick to seize the issue. DEC's effort to eliminate Riverside's pollution of the Blue River has been headed by Bill Fleming.

Riverside readily admits that its effluent from the pulp-making process flows into the Blue. Oyer, an active hunter and fisher, argues that she would never do anything to harm the environment. She contends that residue from the pulp-making process is entirely organic and, therefore, not harmful. Oyer believes, in fact, that the sludge Riverside dumps in the Blue benefits marine life by creating algae. DEC counters that a mildly toxic inorganic chemical is released when pulp is manufactured.

Regardless of its toxicity, however, DEC contends that no discharges should be allowed into the Blue.

The discussions between Fleming and Oyer have become increasingly heated, as the trial date approaches. The issue has also divided the citizens of Forks. Those partial to DEC note the declining salmon yield and a recent increase in bladder disease among Forks' residents. Riverside partisans respond that no causal relationship has been proven regarding either the salmon or the bladder problems. Furthermore, Forks is experiencing high unemployment because of the nationwide decline in the lumber industry; should DEC hurt Riverside's competitive position by imposing penalties, a severe depression might ensue.

Regulations for DEC action derive from the Clean Water Act of 1977, which amended the Federal Water Pollution Control Act of 1972. DEC regulations require existing plants to apply the "best practical control technology currently available." The ambiguity of this clause creates problems, because there are two viable "water scrubbers" on the market: Rotoblue and Technoclean. The latest technology (Technoclean) is unproven and costly, but potentially very powerful. Rotoblue, the current standard, is reliable and less expensive.

DEC has the legal authority to force Riverside to close down until it installs a water scrubber. In addition, DEC could levy a fine against Riverside. A final complication is that some Washington fishermen and a few Forks residents are contemplating suing Riverside for damages caused by pollution in the Blue River. Although Riverside and DEC have probed one another, neither has made a serious offer. With the trial expected to begin in three days, however, Oyer and Fleming have quit grandstanding, and have quietly begun to debate the issues.

2

DEC v. RIVERSIDE

Confidential Instructions for DEC

Although the upcoming lawsuit is of critical importance to Riverside Lumber Company, it is just one of the many crises at the Department of Environmental Conservation (DEC). Bill Fleming, DEC representative in the Riverside affair, considers Riverside, Forks, and even the Blue River to be relatively inconsequential. He is, however, concerned about two aspects of the Riverside case. First, he is less prepared than he would like to be. He realizes that he will need to draw information out of Riverside in order to perform credibly. Second, Fleming does not want to set a bad precedent; Riverside's case will influence environmental standards and enforcement throughout the Pacific Northwest.

In preparation for today's meeting with President Oyer of Riverside Lumber, Fleming drew up this brief summary of his thoughts and intentions.

I. STOP THE DUMPING

Any negotiated agreement must begin with Riverside installing a water scrubber as soon as possible. The Clean Water Act prohibits Riverside's disposal of effluent into the Blue and the dumping must be stopped. The credibility of DEC has been under serious attack of late, and I think a gesture is needed to assuage the criticisms.

II. WHICH TECHNOLOGY SHOULD BE REQUIRED?

There are two types of "water scrubbers" available for use in pulp plants: Rotoblue and Technoclean. Rotoblue is used widely throughout the Pacific Northwest. A $250,000 Rotoblue scrubber suitable for Riverside's needs would eliminate 90% of the particulate matter dumped in the Blue. On the other hand, a $450,000 Technoclean model would eliminate 99.8% of Riverside's particulate emissions. The Technoclean scrubber, however, has never been used on a pulp mill. The consensus, in a meeting of our engineers, was that there is a 20% chance that it will fail entirely. If the Technoclean is purchased and it fails, Riverside should then be required to replace it with the Rotoblue scrubber.

If the Technoclean scrubber works as designed, it will classify as the "best practical control technology currently available," because it eliminates 9.8% more particulate matter than the Rotoblue. Once this standard is established, it will apply to all other pulp mills as well. Unless a pulp manufacturer installs a Technoclean scrubber in the near future, DEC will have to spend $200,000 performing tests on the new scrubber. Therefore, it would be wise to persuade Riverside to install a Technoclean, even at some expense to DEC. One method of assistance would be to "guarantee" the Technoclean scrubber; DEC could pay to replace Riverside's Technoclean with a Rotoblue if the former fails. If challenged by fiscal conservatives, this guarantee could be defended because it effectively tests a new product. An alternative to the guarantee would be to directly subsidize Riverside's purchase of a Technoclean. If DEC subsidizes Riverside, however, other firms will probably demand equal treatment. While it is difficult to estimate the extent of such demands, for the purpose of this negotiation, I will ascribe a total real and imputed cost to DEC of $2 for every $1 of the subsidy. This cost estimate is based on the assumption that subsidies to other companies will increase by approximately $1 for every dollar given to subsidize Riverside's scrubber. The maximum allowable subsidy to Riverside is $450,000, the cost of a Technoclean scrubber. Of course, it is also possible to provide both a subsidy and a guarantee.

If Riverside buys a water scrubber, it can purchase either a Technoclean or a Rotoblue; DEC has the means to influence Riverside's decision. The alternatives facing DEC, and the cost of each option, are outlined in the following table.

THE COST TO DEC OF ITS WATER SCRUBBER OPTIONS

Option	Cost
in $$$s)	
1. Riverside buys a Rotoblue without DEC assistance DEC spends $200,000 testing the Technoclean at another location	200
2. Riverside buys a Technoclean without DEC assistance No DEC testing of Technoclean is required.	0
3. Riverside buys a Technoclean which DEC guarantees Possibility A: Technoclean functions properly, DEC pays nothing. (This outcome has a probability of .8.) Possibility B: Technoclean fails, DEC buys Riverside a Rotoblue. DEC cost = $238,000 (*a) (This outcome has a probability of .2.)	48

2

82

The expected cost of this guarantee is $48,000, which is obtained
by multiplying the cost of each possibility by its probability and adding them together:

($0 X .8) + ($238,000 X .2) = $47,600, which we round off to $48,000

4. Riverside buys a Technoclean which DEC subsidizes   2 X subsidy
The expected cost of the subsidy equals the cost of the subsidy to
Riverside plus an equivalent amount paid to the other firms. (*b)

5. Riverside buys a Technoclean which DEC subsidizes
and guarantees   48 + 2 X subsidy
This is simply the sum of options #3 and #4, above.

6. Riverside does not buy a scrubber   1,000
DEC would need to test the Technoclean. Perhaps Riverside would
be forced to shut down, thereby incurring immense social costs.
If Riverside continues to operate without a scrubber, the precedent
would damage our institutional credibility.

(*a: The Rotoblue purchased to replace the Technoclean actually costs $250,000, not
the $238,000 listed above. However, the purchase is deferred six months (until
Technoclean is installed and fails). The net present value to DEC of $250,000 at a 10%
discount rate, six months in the future is $238,000.

(*b: The subsidy cannot exceed $450,000, the cost of the Technoclean.)

III. LIABILITY FOR DAMAGES CAUSED BY POLLUTION IN THE BLUE

President Oyer has conceded a certain willingness to move toward settlement were it
not for her fear of future damage claims filed by people and firms "injured" by pollution
in the Blue River. She fears that installing a water scrubber might be seen as an
admission that Riverside's pollution has caused the various maladies that have
circulated in the press.

I understand that Riverside has a catastrophe insurance fund with a $550,000
deductible, which covers such liability eventualities. It is within our capacity to assume
some of Riverside's liability, but it has never been done before. If I agree to help cover
some of their anticipated liabilities, other firms may use this precedent to argue for
similar treatment. It is probable that the number of requests for liability assistance from
other polluters will vary directly with the amount of liability assistance paid to Riverside,
because firms will be particularly attracted by large sums of money. For the purposes of
my calculations, I am going to impute costs to DEC according to the values listed in the
table below. (For the purpose of this exercise, these options should be treated as

discrete, not continuous.)

DEC COST OF LIABILITY ASSISTANCE

Amount of liability assistance (in $$$s)	Real and imputed costs (in $$$s)
0	0
50	50
100	110
150	175
200	250
300	390

IV. FORCING RIVERSIDE TO CLOSE

DEC has the legal authority to close down Riverside until it installs a water scrubber. There are several factors to consider before taking such action: 1) shutting down Riverside would illustrate DEC's seriousness and encourage other companies to curtail their pollution; 2) there are social costs to closure which are particularly onerous in this case because Forks is currently experiencing abnormally high unemployment; 3) it might be possible to enhance DEC's credibility without incurring social costs if the mere threat of mandatory closure forces Riverside to purchase a scrubber; 4) perhaps we could close Riverside briefly, but allow it to reopen before the economy of Forks is severely disrupted; and 5) Riverside is currently losing money, so their response to threats of closure is uncertain. Obviously, there are costs and benefits to each alternative facing DEC. The total imputed cost of each option is listed in the table on the following page. (For the purpose of this exercise, these options should be treated as discrete, not continuous.)

5

THE STATUS OF RIVERSIDE LUMBER COMPANY

Status	Imputed Cost to DEC (in $$$s)
1. Riverside remains open. (*a)	0
2. Riverside is closed for 2 months, then allowed to reopen.	50
3. Riverside is closed for six months	200
4. Riverside is closed permanently.	1,100

(*a: It is not necessary to close the plant while the scrubber is being installed.)

V. PUBLIC RELATIONS CAMPAIGN

DEC has a discretionary fund to be used for "public information campaigns." Typically, this money has been used to solidify the support from DEC's allies by getting films of the offenders' pollution to the media. Often the mere threat of such a public relations campaign provides the catalyst for industries to clean up. Of course, the media tactics need not be so negative, they may, in fact, be used to support exemplary firms. For the purpose of this negotiation, we must select one of the following discrete amounts to spend on the public relations campaign: $0, $50,000, $100,000, $150,000, or $200,000.

VI. COMPLIANCE INCENTIVE

This might be a case where DEC could dip into its "compliance incentive" fund, which is used to encourage corporations to install antipollution devices. Typically, these funds are only distributed to projects with a large economic impact; saving Washington's salmon industry might provide a sufficient justification. We have the authority to present money from this fund to a given corporation, subject to certain contingencies which we set. It is, in effect, a reward for good behavior. The compliance incentive funds can be granted in multiples of $50,000 up to the maximum of $200,000. As with liability assistance, however, the combined real and imputed marginal cost of such grants exceeds the real cost, and it increases more rapidly. This effect is caused by the onslaught of corporations which request such funds once the ice has been broken. Thus, we are not eager to set this precedent. My estimate of the effect is presented in the following table:

6

COMPLIANCE INCENTIVE

Amount of Grant (in $$$s)	Real and Imputed Cost (in $$$s)
0	0
50	70
100	160
150	280
200	400

VII. ALTERNATIVE TO A NEGOTIATED SETTLEMENT

If we fail to reach an agreement with Riverside today, the case will be resolved in court. If we win, it will cost us $50,000 in legal fees and we will get a lasting precedent supporting our interpretation of the Clean Water Act. The court, however, may force Riverside to shut down and we would still not have any information about the viability of the Technoclean scrubber. This is a tricky outcome to assess, but I would consider a victory in court to be worth a positive $200,000.

If we lose, on the other hand, it will be a disaster. Our image will suffer, and all our subsequent negotiations with other polluters would be seriously complicated. I think DEC's total imputed cost of losing in court, because of the precedent and the damage to our institutional credibility, would be approximately two million dollars. It would also be a disaster for me personally.

I think it is equally likely that we will win or lose if the case goes to court. For the purpose of the upcoming negotiation with Deborah Oyer, I think I should impute an expected cost, which would reflect all of my concerns, of about $900,000 for going to court. If I am unable to negotiate a deal with Oyer that would cost less than $900,000 in expected real and imputed costs, then I would prefer to go to court.

7

SUMMARY OF DEC'S COSTS
(Do not show this confidential information to the Riverside negotiator)

ISSUE/OPTION	EXPECTED REAL AND IMPUTED COST (in $000s)
I. Which technology: What assistance	
a. Riverside buys a Rotoblue without DEC assistance	200
b. Riverside buys a Technoclean without DEC assistance	0
c. Riverside buys a Technoclean which DEC guarantees	48
d. Riverside buys a Technoclean which DEC subsidizes	2 X subsidy
e. Riverside buys a Technoclean which DEC subsidizes and guarantees	48 + (2 X subsidy)
f. Riverside does not buy a scrubber	1,000
II. Amount of Liability Assistance	
a. 0	0
b. 50	50
c. 100	110
d. 150	175
e. 200	250
f. 300	390
III. Plant Closing	
a. remain open	0
b. close for two months	50
c. close for six months	200
d. closed permanently	1,000
IV. DEC Expenditures for Public Relations	
a. 0	0
b. 50	50
c. 100	100
d. 150	150
e. 200	200
V. Amount of Compliance Incentive	
a. 0	0
b. 50	70
c. 100	160
d. 150	280
e. 200	400
VI. Alternative to a Negotiated Agreement (Go to court)	900

8

SCORING SHEET: DEC

Name:
Opponent:

If settled, please indicate the terms of your final agreement and the cost of your contract.

Issue	Option	Real & Imputed Costs
1. Which technology, if any? Amount of subsidy? Will it be guaranteed?		
2. Will Riverside remain open or closed? (How long if closed?)		
3. Amount spent on public relations.		
4. Amount of liability assistance.		
5. Amount of compliance incentive.		
6. Total real and imputed cost of the contract (sum of lines 1-5)		
7. Savings because of settlement ($900,000*-line 6)		

If you did not settle, please check this box: Impasse:(   )

Rank on a scale of 1 to 10 (with 10 being highest), how well you think you did on this exercise.

(*Note: this number is confidential.)

9

DEC v. RIVERSIDE

Confidential Instructions for Riverside Lumber

MEMORANDUM

TO: Deborah Oyer
FROM: Robert Umlauf
DATE: October 4, of two years ago
RE: Negotiations with Bill Fleming of DEC

In preparation for your meeting with Bill Fleming, you asked me to prepare analysis on the following issues:

1. How important is it that Riverside remain open?
2. Which water scrubber is best for Riverside?
3. Who is liable for damages caused by pollution in the Blue?
4. Are there any public relations tactics we could utilize?
5. Will DEC provide us with compliance assistance funds?

You also asked me to spare you the details; you wanted the bottom line on each of the above items. Well, I appreciate your confidence, but I could not resist including some of my assumptions and calculations. The figures presented hereinafter represent Riverside's estimated net after-tax costs. Investment tax credits and depreciation allowances have been factored in when appropriate, and all figures have been discounted to account for the time value of money.

I. HOW IMPERATIVE IS IT THAT RIVERSIDE REMAIN OPEN?

If Riverside were operating profitably, it would be to our advantage to remain open. At this time, however, Riverside is losing money because of slumps in the construction and lumber industries. There are four possible agreements which could be made with DEC on the question of our remaining open: 1) remain open; 2) close for two months (this would be a compromise solution to appease DEC's constituency); 3) close for six months (until the scrubber is installed); and, 4) close permanently. Here are my estimates of our profitability under each alternative:

1. Remain open: Total cost = $200,000
It is estimated that we could return to profitability in four months, but we would lose $200,000 in

the meantime. As mentioned above, all of these calculations include tax considerations.

2. Close for two months: Total cost = $100,000
We could deplete our inventories while actively soliciting sales. By running a stripped-down operation which eliminates variable costs, we would hold our losses to only $100,000.

3. Close for six months: Total cost = $150,000
As in 2 above, we could build up a backlog of orders that would be an asset down the road. By the end of six months, however, we would have no inventory, no income, and losses would begin to climb.

4. Close permanently: Total cost = $7,000,000
Although the short-run outlook for Riverside and the lumber industry is poor, the long-range picture is much better. If we bail out now, we will have substantial foregone opportunities.

II. WHICH WATER SCRUBBER IS BEST FOR RIVERSIDE?

There are two types of water scrubbers available for use in pulp plants: Rotoblue and Technoclean. Rotoblue is widely used throughout the Pacific Northwest. A $250,000 Rotoblue scrubber suitable for Riverside's needs would eliminate 90% of the effluent dumped in the Blue. On the other hand, a $450,000 Technoclean would eliminate 99.8% of our particulate emissions. The Technoclean scrubber, however, has never been used on a pulp mill; our actuaries estimate a 20% chance that it will fail entirely. If Technoclean is purchased and it fails, Riverside would then be required to replace it with the Rotoblue scrubber. The expected cost of a Technoclean scrubber, given the possibility of failure (minus the forestalled environmental costs as outlined below), is $497,000 (see Appendix I, attached).

It is ironic that, in resolving one legal problem with DEC, we might create conditions that would soon embroil us in another. That is, several environmental groups have stated that they will sue us if, in an out-of-court settlement with DEC, we agree to anything other than the installation of Technoclean. In assessing this threat, I believe that, if we do not install a scrubber, the environmentalists will almost certainly sue. They would not, however, be expected to sue if we install Technoclean (though they could go after past damages), and it is uncertain how vigorously they would pursue a suit if we were to go with a Rotoblue.

The cost of battling the environmentalists (following our suit with DEC) is expected to vary with our choice of scrubber as follows: if we do not install a scrubber, our legal and associated costs will total $200,000; if we buy a Rotoblue, the legal fees will drop to $100,000; and if we install a Technoclean, we will avoid these suits altogether. Therefore, the net cost (purchase price plus legal fees) of the Technoclean is $497,000, the Rotoblue is $350,000, and doing nothing is $200,000.

If we decide to purchase a Technoclean, DEC might be willing to share some of our expenses,

2

because we would be helping them by testing an untried product. DEC could guarantee the Technoclean, agreeing to pay for a Rotoblue as a replacement should the former fail. With a guarantee, our cost for purchasing a Technoclean would fall from $497,000 to $450,000. (This $450,000 figure is calculated as follows: the Technoclean costs $450,000. But, in the event of a Technoclean failure, DEC would be required to buy a Rotoblue to replace it. Thus, our costs would simply be $450,000.) DEC might also be willing to pay some of our costs directly (they could provide this subsidy with or without the guarantee). If so, our costs would equal $497,000 (or, $450,000 if guaranteed) minus the amount of the subsidy.

III. WHAT IS RIVERSIDE'S LIABILITY FOR DAMAGES CAUSED BY POLLUTION IN THE BLUE?

There are persistent rumors that Riverside is about to be hit with a rash of suits from the fishing industry because of the declining salmon yield, and from Forks citizens with bladder diseases. If we install a water scrubber, it could be interpreted as an admission of guilt; in any case, our potential legal costs and damage payments could reach astronomical proportions. Fortunately, we have "catastrophe insurance" with a $550,000 deductible, which covers events such as pollution damage suits. After factoring in the probability of being sued, the distribution of possible awards, the amount of insurance we carry, and the effect of such claims on our taxes, the total cost of our liability is expected to equal $270,000. (The net after-tax cost of Riverside's liability, should total liabilities exceed $550,000, would be only $300,000 because deductibles can be expensed. It should not, however, be assumed that liabilities will surpass this figure; Riverside could win some of the suits or perhaps only a few will be filed. We should, therefore, discount our total expected liability from $300,000 to $270,000. For the purposes of this exercise, consider the liability costs to be fixed at $270,000.)

We may also be able to convince DEC to pay us a lump sum, which will cover part of our expected liability. Unfortunately, the tax implications are such that DEC payments for liability coverage are only worth $ .54 to the dollar. That is, every dollar of liability assistance from DEC increases our taxes by $ .46, so the net gain is only $ .54. (See table)

3

Net Gain from DEC Liability Assistance

Amount of DEC Liability Assistance:	Riverside's Expected Liability (in $$$s) After receiving DEC assistance: (in $000s)
	(Liability = 270 - (.54 X DEC assistance)
0	270
50	243
100	216
150	189
200	162
300	108

IV. Public Relations

After battling DEC, the environmental groups, and the fishing industry for three full years, Riverside has lost considerable public esteem. Unfortunately, we have been "in the red" for so long, that an advertising campaign aimed at restoring public opinion would be prohibitively expensive. If we cooperate with DEC and eliminate our pollution of the Blue, however, they might do us a favor in return. Perhaps Riverside, if it were depicted as a "model corporation" using the latest anti-pollution technology, could be the centerpiece of a DEC-sponsored media campaign in the Pacific Northwest. Conversely, if our discussions become antagonistic, DEC might sponsor a negative campaign, which could further damage our profitability.

It is expected that a media campaign of this nature would boost sales of our pulp somewhat. Even if the public relations effort does not translate directly into increased sales, it would definitely have non-economic benefits, such as improving our "goodwill" in the community. The initial money would be extremely worthwhile in overcoming the public disdain for Riverside; the marginal benefit, however, would decrease as additional resources are allocated to public relations. Our imputed return, as a function of DEC expenditures for a public relations campaign on behalf of Riverside, is indicated in the following table: (Imputed returns are those which are attributed to a cause, even if the linkage is somewhat indirect.)

4

PUBLIC RELATIONS

Type of Campaign/DEC Expenditure: (in $000s)	Resulting Increase in Riverside's Profitability: (in $$$s)
Negative/Any amount	(200)
Positive/0	0
Positive/50	75
Positive/100	100
Positive/150	120
Positive/200	130

V. COMPLIANCE INCENTIVE

I understand that DEC has a "compliance incentive" fund, but I don't know too much about it. Apparently they are able to provide grants in multiples of $50,000 up to $200,000, to reward firms which install anti-pollution devices. DEC's criteria for distribution from this fund is somewhat hazy, but it will probably be worth our while to request a compliance incentive grant. The burden of proof, undoubtedly, will be on us to convince DEC that Riverside deserves these funds.

VI. ALTERNATIVE TO A NEGOTIATED AGREEMENT

If we fail to reach an agreement with DEC today, the case will be resolved in court. Appendix II, attached, indicates that our expected cost of going to court is roughly $640,000. If you could negotiate a deal with Fleming that would cost less than this amount in expected real and imputed costs, then you should avoid going to court. Your bottom line, therefore, is to negotiate a contract that would result in expected real and imputed costs as much below $640,000 as possible.

5

SUMMARY OF RIVERSIDE'S COSTS
(Do not show this confidential information to the DEC negotiator)

ISSUE/OPTION	EXPECTED REAL & IMPUTED COSTS (revenue in $000s)
1. Should Riverside remain open, or should it close?	
a) remain open	200
b) close for 2 months	100
c) close for 6 months	150
d) close permanently	7,000
2. Which Water Scrubber?*	
a) Riverside buys a Rotoblue	350
b) We buy a Technoclean without DEC assistance	497
c) We buy a Technoclean which DEC guarantees	450
d) We buy a Technoclean which DEC subsidizes	497-subsidy
e) We buy a Technoclean which DEC subsidizes and guarantees	450-subsidy
f) We do not buy a scrubber (but incur costs related to continued legal battles)	200
3. Amount of DEC Liability Assistance	
a) 0	270
b) 50	243
c) 100	216
d) 150	189
e) 200	162
f) 300	108
4. Public Relations (type of campaign/amount of DEC public relations)	
a) negative/any amount	200
b) none/0	0
c) positive/50	(75)
d) positive/100	(100)
e) positive/150	(120)
f) positive/200	(130)

6

5. <u>Amount of DEC compliance incentive</u>

a) 0	0
b) 50	(50)
c) 100	(100)
d) 150	(150)
e) 200	(200)

6. <u>Alternative to a negotiated agreement (court)</u> 640

*Scrubber costs include purchase price and expected legal fees related to choice of technology.

7

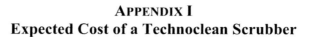

APPENDIX I
Expected Cost of a Technoclean Scrubber

There are three essential factors involved in determining the expected $497,000 cost of purchasing a Technoclean scrubber:

    1. the purchase price of the scrubber,
    2. the probability that Technoclean will function properly,
    3. the discounted cost of replacing the Technoclean with a Rotoblue if the former fails.

Possibility A: Technoclean functions properly: Cost = $450,000

    This $450,000 expense is simply the purchase price of the Technoclean scrubber.

    (According to our actuarial estimates, this outcome has a probability of .8)

Possibility B: Technoclean fails, Riverside buys a Rotoblue: Cost = $686,000

As in Possibility A, we buy Technoclean at $450,000. If Technoclean fails, we will replace it with a Rotoblue for a "present value" expense of $236,000.
(**note below) The total cost is the sum of these two costs.

    (This outcome has a probability of .2)

Combining the two possibilities:

The expected cost of purchasing a Technoclean, then, is $497,000, which is obtained by multiplying the cost of each possibility by its probability and then adding:

    ($450,000 X .8) + ($686,000 X .2) = $497,000

(**Note: The Rotoblue purchased to replace the Technoclean actually costs $250,000, not the $236,000 listed above. Because the purchase is deferred six months (until Technoclean is installed and it fails), the $250,000 cost to Riverside should be discounted six months at a rate of 12%, to $236,000.)

    8

APPENDIX II
Expected Cost of Going to Court

The estimated cost of going to court against DEC on the pollution case would be $637,000. This, as usual, is an after-tax figure; tax credits, depreciation, and discounting have already been factored into the solution. My estimate is predicated on the belief that there are four possible outcomes to the case:

      1. Riverside wins
      2. Riverside loses, low cost
      3. Riverside loses, medium cost
      4. Riverside loses, high cost

I have developed scenarios to fit each outcome. From these potential scenarios, I determined the cost to Riverside of each option, then I consulted our lawyers, who estimated the probability of each outcome transpiring. Given this information, it was possible to determine the expected cost of litigation:
[expected cost = (cost 1 X probability 1) + (cost 2 X probability 2) + (cost 3 X probability 3) + (cost 4 X probability 4)]. The following table displays my model of the possible courtroom solutions and costs.

9

POSSIBLE COURT DECISIONS

Outcome/Riverside expenses	Item Cost	Total Cost (in $000s)	Probability (in $000s)
1) Riverside wins			
Riverside:			
a) has legal expenses; and	$20		
b) remains open (but loses money for 4 months)	200		
Total	$220		.5
2) Riverside loses; low cost			
Riverside:			
a) has legal expenses	$20		
b) is required to install a Rotoblue	250		
c) remains open (but loses money for 4 months); and	200		
d) is fined	500		
Total	$970		.2
3) Riverside loses; medium cost			
Riverside:			
a) has legal expenses	$20		
b) is required to install a Rotoblue	250		
c) is temporarily shut down 6 months; and	250		
d) is fined	500		
Total	$1,020		.2

10

100

4) **Riverside loses; high cost**

Riverside:

a) has legal expenses	$20	
b) is required to install a Rotoblue	250	
c) is temporarily shut down 6 months; and	250	
d) is fined; and	500	
e) is responsible for future liability claims	<u>270</u>	
Total	$1,290	.1

Scoring Sheet: Riverside

Name:
Opponent:

If settled, please indicate the terms of your final agreement and the cost of your contract.

Issue	Option	Real & Imputed Costs
1. Which technology, if any? Amount of subsidy? Will it be guaranteed?		
2. Will Riverside remain open or closed? (How long if closed?)		
3. Amount spent on public relations.		
4. Amount of liability assistance.		
5. Amount of compliance incentive.		
6. Total real and imputed cost of the contract (sum of lines 1-5)		
7. Savings because of settlement ($640,000***- line 6)		

If you did not settle, please check this box: Impasse:( )

Rank on a scale of 1 to 10 (with 10 being highest), how well you think you did on this exercise.

***Note:** this number is confidential

12